TURKEY

TURKEY
WHAT EVERYONE NEEDS TO KNOW

ANDREW FINKEL

OXFORD
UNIVERSITY PRESS

OXFORD

UNIVERSITY PRESS

Oxford University Press, Inc., publishes works that further
Oxford University's objective of excellence
in research, scholarship, and education.

Oxford   New York
Auckland   Cape Town   Dar es Salaam   Hong Kong   Karachi
Kuala Lumpur   Madrid   Melbourne   Mexico City   Nairobi
New Delhi   Shanghai   Taipei   Toronto

With offices in
Argentina   Austria   Brazil   Chile   Czech Republic   France   Greece
Guatemala   Hungary   Italy   Japan   Poland   Portugal   Singapore
South Korea   Switzerland   Thailand   Turkey   Ukraine   Vietnam

Published by Oxford University Press, Inc.
198 Madison Avenue, New York, NY 10016
www.oup.com

Oxford is a registered trademark of Oxford University Press.

Library of Congress Cataloging-in-Publication Data

Finkel, Andrew, 1953–
Turkey : what everyone needs to know / Andrew Finkel.
p. cm.
ISBN 978–0–19–973304–0 (pbk. : alk. paper) — ISBN 978–0–19–973305–7 (alk. paper)
1. Turkey—History.   2. Turkey—Civilization.   3. Turkey—Politics and government.
4. Turkey—Economic conditions.   I. Title.
DR440.F56 2012
956.1—dc23
2011044539

1 3 5 7 9 8 6 4 2

Printed in the United States of America
on acid-free paper

CONTENTS

ACKNOWLEDGMENTS

Coincidence is the catalyst of many an enterprise. The idea to write this book was brought to me by Howard Morhaim, whose literary agency is a short ride to where my grandfather taught high-school history in Brooklyn, yet whose own ancestors are buried within sight of my Istanbul home. I am grateful for his curiosity about Turkey that initiated this book and to a friend, the historian Günhan Börekçi, for effecting the introduction. Tim Bent of Oxford University Press saw the project through with good humor and patience, ably assisted by Keely Latcham.

My own first tutorial in the essentials of Turkey came many years ago at the hands of Güzin Berkmen, a pioneer of teaching Turkish to foreigners. She taught not just the structure of the language but the more illusive grammar of everyday life. Like all her students, I cherish her memory. Since then, many friends have done their best to educate me and discuss or respond to my questions; and still others I have imagined standing over my shoulder, reading the text with a skeptical eye. Among those on whose generosity and judgement I have come to rely are Mensur Akgün, Şahin Alpay, İzak Atiyas, Gökhan Bacik, Yavuz Baydar, Alkis Courcoulas,

Yorgos Dedes, Selim Deringil, Mehmet Ali Dikerdem, Joe Duran, Edhem Eldem, Seljuk Esenbel, Maureen Freely, Mehmet Gerz, Ioannis Grigoriadis, Murat Güvenç, Joost Lagendijk, Michael Lake, Heath Lowry, William Hale, Aliza Marcus, John McCarthy, Metin Münir, Ahmed Pekın, Hugh Pope, Scott Redford, Yigal Schleifer, John Scott, and Nükhet Sirman. Sıtkı Kösemen spent time trying to take a flattering author's photograph. Ali Öz, Ahmet Polat, and Clive Crook also deserve thanks for offering aesthetic advice. Sinan Kurmuş, Alessandra Ricci, and Murat Üçer read and commented on specific sections related to their disciplines. Hrant Dink both in his life and through his untimely death asked questions of Turkish society, and the memory of our conversations invests some sections of this book.

Anita Sinclair read an early version of the manuscript and cheered me on. So did Izzy Finkel. The thanks I owe the latter are not for her filial devotion but a merciless attention to detail. It is a trait she inherited through the distaff side. My wife, Caroline Finkel, is possessed of an academic method that has provided a safety line to my journalistic flights of fancy. That she is a first-rate historian of the Ottoman Empire is an additional bit of good luck. Essentialisms and broad generalizations that have made it to the final cut are my own responsibility.

A final word of thanks belongs to my parents, Dorothy and Lee Finkel, who brought me to live in Turkey at a time when this was an unfashionably eccentric thing to do. Why they did so is a question with no precise answer, but it is to my parents and their adventurous decision that I dedicate this book.

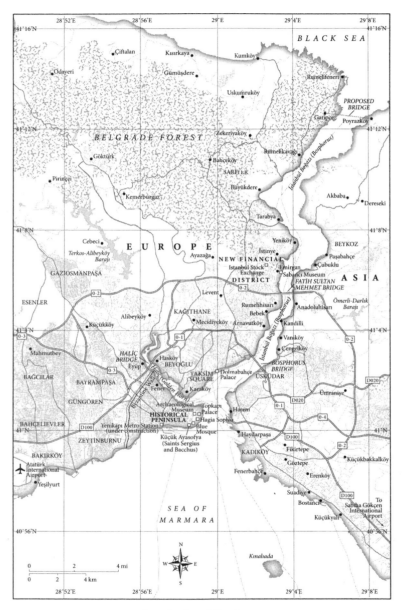

Istanbul and Environs

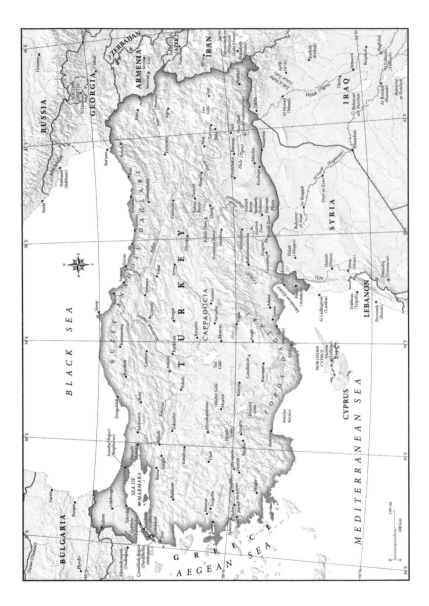

1
INTRODUCTION

Why this book?

The method of this book is to investigate a complex subject succinctly by posing a series of questions that beg answers that beget more questions. It is hard to squeeze an introduction into such a scheme unless the very first question is, "Why did you write this book?" That, of course, is the most awkward question of all, since anyone setting out to produce an account of modern Turkey has an uncomfortable sense of being about to commit perjury. Perhaps all truisms have a mirage-like tendency to evaporate the closer one approaches and it would be foolish to pretend that Turkey is uniquely inscrutable. However, as a journalist working in Turkey for over two decades, I have learned from hard experience the challenge of writing news stories with shelf-lives longer than a week, let alone producing generalities that will nestle comfortably on a bedside table. Turkey is a society in the throes of enormous change, and any snapshot of the here-and-now is bound to be blurred.

Nonetheless, I believe a book can locate the underlying reasons for this fast-moving dynamic, some of which will reveal my own motives for embarking on this hazardous project. I first moved to Istanbul for a year in 1967, a schoolboy in tow to his parents. Philadelphia, where I was born, was then a city of two million people. Like many American cities, it has since shed population and now has 1.5 million people—approximately the size of the Istanbul I first encountered over forty years ago. Today, Istanbul is a megacity of well over 13 million people, the lion's share of that growth fueled by the in-migration of people in search of a better life. At the height of its expansion in 1970, the population of Istanbul increased every year by what elsewhere would be regarded as a decent-sized city in its own right (over 300,000 annually: think Cardiff or Toledo). By 2009 the rate of increase had slowed to a mere 1.7 percent, but that still amounts to 218,000 people. And what was true for Istanbul has been true for other Turkish cities. In 1945 a quarter of the population was urban; that figure is closer to 70 percent now. In France, one of Europe's most rural societies, 77 percent of the population is urban, suggesting that in Turkey this transition has not fully run its course.

In Washington, the realization that there was something about Turkey that the United States government did not fully understand dawned very suddenly when, on March 1, 2003, the Turkish parliament denied the U.S. military the right to launch a northern front from Turkish territory in the imminent war in Iraq. The Pentagon, the U.S. Congress, and the media watched openmouthed as Turkey, once the most stalwart of NATO members, behaved like Atlas setting down his load. Had Turkey suddenly renounced the Western orientation on which the Republic was founded as well as its own strategic importance to its allies? An answer of sorts came a year later when the government in Ankara clawed through a process of reform to win the right to begin accession talks with the European Union. Even more confusing was that the government which showed such strength of purpose was led by a charismatic prime minister who had cut his political teeth in a pro-Islamic and anti-Western political movement. Was his conversion a Nixon-in-China realpolitik epiphany or a cynical attempt to outflank Turkey's secularist establishment? What, if anything, had changed?

Any study of Turkey trying to answer the concerns of an English-speaking audience must address how an ever-more-powerful nation, in which almost the entire population is born into the Muslim faith, allies itself in the world. Will Turkey continue to act as the self-declared bridge between East and West in the new century? And can it complete a process of democratic reform and create the opportunities and prosperity an increasingly informed citizenry has come to expect? These are all wise questions. Yet the subtext of my own enquiry is whatever happened to the Istanbul I knew as a youth.

I returned to Turkey as a journalist in 1989, the year in which the Soviet Empire imploded. In May of that year, some months before the toppling of the Berlin Wall, I stood in a refugee camp inside the Turkish-Bulgarian border that was trying to accommodate some of the 300,000 Bulgarian Turks who had fled from the last gasp of tyrannical discrimination during the regime of Todor Zhikov—the party boss who had ruled his country since 1954. It was impossible not to conclude that while the bankruptcy of Soviet ideology may have been the motor of change, the uncontrolled movement of population was steering events. In 1991, at the end of the First Gulf War, I climbed a mountain on the other side of the country, on Turkey's border with Iraq, and witnessed what seemed a biblical spectacle—an exodus of hundreds of thousands of Iraqi Kurdish refugees trudging through snow, trying to keep a step ahead of Saddam Hussein's Republican Guard. In 1999, I was back in the first refugee camp, near Bulgaria, now filled with Albanian Kosovars who had been airlifted from a mud-sodden no man's land along the Macedonian border. In 2011, Turkey prepared to meet yet another wave of refugees in its southeast as the al-Assad regime in Syria imploded into civil war.

If Turkey seems surrounded by other people's history, then it was in the center of a transformation of its own. To put it at its simplest, the city where I live has, during my lifetime, doubled in population, then doubled again, and then doubled a third time. That in the process no regime collapsed and no walls fell has only made Turkish society harder to read. The story of postwar Turkish society is that of the social impulses and political responses generated by this huge movement of people. This helps, too, to give a point of reference for those unfamiliar with Turkey. Saul Bellow's 1953 novel *The Adventures of Augie March*, set in the Chicago Depression, describes a tough world of hustle, hardships, and opportunity that is not a far cry from the big Turkish cities of the 1970s. By the same token, anyone trying to grapple with the threat posed by a popular Islamic revival of the 1990s could first consider the rise of Methodism or Nonconformism during the British industrial revolution. Protestant "fundamentalism" was seen as a militant challenge to the established orthodoxy, though in retrospect it appears to have been a deeply conservative force, famously providing a work ethic, support network, and sense of purpose to the urban poor and emerging middle class, as well as reconciling individuals to social change.

Turkey's own ability to remember is affected by its youthful demographic. Half the population is under twenty-nine years of age. An "average" Turk, therefore, would have been born after the 1980 military coup and might recall growing up in a country dominated by the Motherland Party of Turgut Özal, who came to power when the country returned to civilian rule in 1983. Mr. Özal is remembered as a visionary who accelerated Turkish integration into the global economy. Alas, his party no longer exists, imploding of its own accord. Turkish university students born in 1990 can be forgiven for not remembering who was in power during their formative decade, since there were eleven separate coalition governments made up from parties of which all but one or two have disappeared from the political scene. A schoolchild born in 2000 is one year older than the party governing Turkey at the time this book is being written.

The Turkish economy has followed an even steeper roller-coaster ride. Beginning in 1970, the country suffered from the rare malaise of chronic inflation. Throughout the 1990s prices rose on average 72 percent per year, enough to require a 20 million lira note but not enough to result in hyperinflation (as in the German Weimar Republic of the 1920s when shoppers needed a wheelbarrow instead of a wallet). My monthly university salary in 1982 was not enough to buy a loaf of bread by the end of that decade. Not surprisingly, for most of Turkey's postwar history there was no such thing as a mortgage. Who on earth could estimate the rate of repayment on even a medium-term loan? In the United States or Europe, home loans are equal to or even greater than the GDP. In Turkey, home loans are still negligible—some 5 percent of GDP. Foreign banks have, therefore, been queuing up to get into the Turkish market now that inflation and interest rates have become relatively stable. Yet despite the absence of long-term credit, rates of home ownership are at around 70 percent, a figure comparable to that in the United States (in conditions of instability, people will do anything to own their own home). In the United States, an underregulated mortgage market created a cycle of boom and all-too-dramatic bust. Turkey might emulate that treacherous path and yet a well-regulated mortgage market could be the ticket to economic parity with the European Union it aspires to join. The question of "why does Turkey matter" pertains not simply to defense analysts; the investment community ignores at its peril the fastest-growing credit card market in Europe. UN projections suggest the Turkish population, currently at over 75 million, will stabilize at around 95 million by 2050 but that by 2025 it will already be greater than that projected for Germany. Yet today, Turkey consumes less than Holland (population less than 17 million), so it is a market that has to be watched.

What will Turkey look like tomorrow? The simple (if unhelpful) answer is, not like it looks today. But the appearance of even dramatic change can be deceptive. Several years ago, I returned to the street in the Philadelphia suburb where I grew up. I felt like an character in an Ingmar Bergman film, returning to a perfectly preserved memory in black and white. It so happens that I have a view from my house in Istanbul westward across the Bosphorus Strait—from Asia to Europe—to the hillside where I first lived over forty years ago. My 1967 house no longer exists; in its place is the footprint of a vast suspension bridge (the fourth-longest in the world, and the longest outside the United States) that links the two continents. Its elegant span, when completed in 1973, became an instant symbol of Turkish modernization.

Calling Istanbul "a bridge between civilizations" became the city's favorite metaphor. Before too long, however, the

Bosphorus Bridge acquired a less flattering reputation in urban planning literature for generating the very problems it was meant to solve. The bridge opened up the city to urban sprawl and traffic gridlock that the authorities could not even pretend to control. So in 1988, Istanbul welcomed a second Fatih Sultan (Mehmet, the Conqueror) Bridge across the Bosphorus to patch up all the problems created by the first. This bridge was meant to allow intercity traffic bypass Istanbul altogether. Commuting traffic would go over the first bridge; long-distance traffic would go over the second. Even before the inaugural ribbon on the second bridge was snipped, however, there was a vast amount of speculative real-estate investment on the Asian side of the bridge. Huge unplanned neighborhoods began to take root. Twenty years on, an infinitesimal portion of the second bridge's traffic is intercity, and the pace of urbanization along its route has been seven times that of elsewhere in a city that has already grown exponentially. Now there are plans for a third bridge.

So if Turkey appears to many a place of extraordinary change, others speak of a country where some things remain depressingly the same. Many of the questions Turkey asks itself have been slow to find answers. Can the evolving demands of Turkey's large Kurdish population be resolved within a rigid constitutional framework that enshrines Turkish nationalism? Can Turkey reach a stasis between government and opposition, politics and military? Can it understand its own history in a way that offers the prospect of reconciliation with its neighbor in Armenia?

Turkey's response to these questions has consequences for the rest of the world. The debates that rage at home resonate well beyond its frontiers. For example, its application to become part of the European Union challenges the notion of

European identity and poses the question of where Europe ends. In 1950, Turkey made a peaceful transition from a single-party regime to a multiparty democracy. Yet subsequent military coups and the Turkish military's continued opposition to an Islamic-leaning government cast doubt on how deep the country's democratic roots run. Does Turkey hold the antidote to religious polarization or is it itself becoming a battleground in the clash of civilizations? Is Turkey's new self-confidence an example for the world or is it leading the country into hubris and isolation?

Questions, questions. Although I have tried to confine myself to what everyone needs to know about Turkey, what has kept me attached to this country all these years is that I wander through this maze of ever more elusive answers.

What is a Turk?

"Happy is the one who says, 'I am a Turk,'" is the much-quoted maxim of a much-quoted man. Mustafa Kemal Atatürk, Turkey's founding president, uttered the words as the emotional finale to a speech in 1933, marking the tenth anniversary of the Republic. It is a simple idea ("if you think you're Turkish, then you are") that belies a sophisticated approach to nation-building. You become a Turk by feeling the benefits and obligations of being a citizen of the Republic of Turkey. In historical context, Atatürk's emphasis on Turkishness was a way of forging an inclusive national identity out of disparate parts. In this, he was very successful. Today, Turkish nationalism is a very powerful force. At the time, even the name for the new state, *Türkiye*, was borrowed from Italian.

Prior to the foundation of the Republic, the word "Turk," although used by the rest of Europe to refer to the sultan's domains, referred to one of the many ethnicities of the Ottoman Empire. Members of a pre-nineteenth-century elite would have been as pleased to be labeled a "Turk" as they would have been to be called a "country bumpkin." A growing pride in Turkishness mirrored the success of other nationalisms—Greek, Slav, Armenian, and Arab—in creating a new loyalty distinct from empire. So to be a Turk was to fight the other nationalist fires with fire. The opposite strategy, Ottomanism, was fealty to a monarch and a state that transcended religion or ethnicity. This was a doomed idea in Europe at the time of the World War I. The very first clause of the Treaty of Lausanne (1923), which called the Republic into existence, also called for the compulsory exchange of the bulk of the Muslim living in Greece with the Greek Orthodox population of Turkey living outside Istanbul. The early twentieth century was an era of racial confrontation, not multiculturalism.

Religion was very much a component of Balkan and Caucasian nationalisms. The autocephalous Orthodox churches in Greece, Bulgaria, and Serbia still play a powerful political role in the states they inspired. Islam also played a role in nascent Turkish nationalism. Influential literary figures like Namik Kemal (1840–1888), who pioneered the use of a written vernacular Turkish language, also regarded Islam and nation as closely intertwined. However, the Republic was determined to break the power of religion, which it regarded as a prop of the sultanic regime. "Turkishness" therefore represented a new kind of social cohesion, one based on popular sovereignty and the defense of well-defined territory. It did not exclude faith as one of its components. In a clause in the 1924 Constitution Islam appears as the official religion, but the clause was deleted four years later. Article 66 of the 1982 Constitution continues to define a "Turk" merely in terms of the bonds of citizenship, and all citizens regardless of creed or gender enjoy equality under the law. By contrast, in everyday parlance, the appellation "Turk" is reserved for someone whose native language is Turkish and who is born into the Muslim faith. This immediately creates ambiguity, since it implies there are Turkish citizens who at some level are not really "Turks."

The obvious examples are non-Muslims (Greeks, Jews, Syriac Christians, and Armenians) whom that same Treaty of Lausanne recognizes as "minorities." Minorities are official anomalies, tolerated exceptions to the one-size-fits-all national identity. Turkish officialdom finds it almost impossible to accept that non-Muslim citizens could confine their principal loyalty to the Turkish state. Ask an ethnic Greek or Jewish or Armenian Turk whether they could become a commissioned officer, a state-appointed provincial governor, or even a diplomat, and they would regard it as a silly question, even though there are no statutes forbidding their entry into these professions.

However, there have been minority Members of Parliament (MPs,) and in 2010 an ethnic Armenian Turk passed a public examination to be accepted as a member of Turkey's EU delegation. Whether these are examples of breakthroughs, window dressing, or exceptions proving the rule is perhaps no longer a pressing issue since the number of non-Muslim Turkish citizens is in decline. Non-Muslims made up a plurality of the population in Istanbul in 1900 (56%). This fell to 35 percent just before the start of World War II. Now minorities are estimated at below 250,000 nationwide in a population of an estimated 75 million people.

Far more problematic are Kurds, whose anomalous status could not be officially recognized. Atatürk's promise of happiness for those who call themselves "Turks" was until recently carved into the hillside opposite the citadel city of Mardin in the southeast of the country, where ethnic Turks are a minority. It seemed a warning that the region's Kurds (and many Arabs) would be a great deal happier not trying to assert a rival identity. Public life does not discriminate against ethnic Kurds who choose to assimilate. Of the eleven Turkish presidents, three have been of Kurdish origin. However, it would be surprising if one in a thousand of their compatriots today could list all three names, given that this ethnicity was never openly referred to.[1]

The issue is complicated still further by the fact that in English there is a distinction between the terms "Turk," and "Turkic" (or sometimes "Turcoman")—the first relating to Turkey while the latter term is a racial and linguistic characteristic of tribal peoples from Central Asia (some of whom migrated into what is now Turkey). In Turkish, there is no such difference, and the expression "Turkish Republics" includes faraway Uzbekistan or Turkmenistan as well as Azerbaijan. The symbol of the Turkish presidency is comprised of a sixteen-point star surrounded by sixteen other stars, each one representing historic Turkic kingdoms (the earliest being the Great Hun Empire from 200 B.C., which stretched from Siberia to Tibet, and the last being the Ottoman Empire founded in A.D. 1299), hinting at a racial side to Turkish identity.

In practice (i.e., if you look at their DNA), Turkish citizens do not make up a distinct ethnic group. Some possess genes that have made the long journey from Central Asia but in far fewer numbers than the cultural and linguistic evidence would suggest. Others owe their parentage to the many migrations into Asia Minor, including the army of Alexander the Great, or the flight of refugees from the Balkans and the Caucasus during the nineteenth century. Still others can trace their gene pool to Bronze Age burial remains found not far from their front doors. So while there are ultranationalists who identify with Turkic origins, others find this atavistic quest embarrassing.

It is certainly the case, however, that Turks are fiercely patriotic, although most would confine that loyalty to the boundaries of the nation-state. Article 301 of the Turkish penal code infamously makes "insulting Turkishness" an offense—but what "Turkishness" means will always be open to interpretation. Increasingly, if not always consistently, Atatürk's maxim is being rethought as the saying, "Happy is the one who says, 'I am a citizen of the Republic of Turkey.'"

Alas, even this assertion is not entirely borne out by an Organization for Economic Co-operation and Development (OECD) survey, which measured how satisfied people from member nations are with their lives. The 2009 OECD report, titled "Society at a Glance," put Turks well below the median— more cheerful than Italians and Slovaks, but far less happy than Scandinavians. The ratio of those who see the glass half-full to those who see it half-empty is generally 1:1. On the other hand, Turks are considerably more sociable than any other of the economically advanced thirty-one OECD members, tending to spend 35 percent of their leisure time with friends. Perhaps what Atatürk meant to say was that Turks are never happier than when getting together to complain.

What sort of language is Turkish?

Turkish might not seem the easiest language to learn— unless you are already fluent in another Altaic language, the linguistic group associated with the Turkic peoples of Central Asia. Even then, the differences are profound. Someone parachuted into Ashkabad or Tashkent from Istanbul would not be able to launch into an after-dinner speech. It is estimated that some 200 million people speak a form of Turkish, but Azerbaijan is the one country where a Turk from Turkey could hold a reasonable conversation. The Turkish of Turkey is spoken in Northern Cyprus, and there are comprehensible dialects spoken in the Balkans, including in Grecian Thrace, Kosovo, and Bulgaria, as well among the Turkmens of Iraq and Syria. Turkish pop songs and television series are popular throughout a wider region, which means that the influence of "standard" Turkish is on the rise.

Turkish is distinctive in that it agglutinates—it adds particles of meaning to the end of the word ("It would appear they are not coming," for example, is all one word). It works on a system of vowel harmony, meaning that suffixes depend on the sound of the preceding syllable. Modern Turkish was sculpted by grammarians meeting in committee so there are few exceptions to the rules. Turks are generally forgiving of foreigners mangling their language, and this civility means in practice that reaching the first plateau of simple comprehensibility is relatively straightforward. The syntax of complex sentences (literally translated, the sentence "the book my assistant gave you about the Turkish economy has not yet been put on the shelf" is "assistant-of mine's to you giving the Turkish economy about book yet shelf-onto put-not-has-been") takes longer to master and, so far, Google Translate has not got the hang of it.

Turkey reinvented its language in 1928, when, in the course of a few months, the Arabic script used to write Ottoman Turkish was replaced with the Latin alphabet. Schoolchildren have not regretted the decision. Turkish functions according to vowel harmony; Arabic cursive script usually omits vowels and was never the perfect medium for transcribing the spoken language. Many words were spelled as they would have been in Persian or Arabic and not how they were pronounced in Turkey, and many Turkish sounds had more than one Arabic equivalent. The new transcription was completely phonetic, spoken exactly as written (inspired by an abortive plan to romanize the Turkic languages of the Soviet Union), and proved an aid to literacy.

The letters *w*, *x*, and *q* are absent in Turkish. These are letters which are used in Latinized Kurdish and deeply frowned upon. Were I to take Turkish citizenship I would be expected to omit the "w" from my first name on the compulsory identity card. Instead, diacritics to Latin letters—such as to the *ı* (dotless i)—accommodate Turkish sounds. Most English-language publications find these diacritics too confusing and in the interests of consistency omit diacritics altogether. If these publications use diacritics that readers might recognize, like the cedillas and umlauts, as in *ç* (pronounced "ch" not "s" as in *français)* or *ü*, you would logically have to use the ones unique to Turkish that most readers don't know— such as *ş* (for a "sh" sound) or *ğ* (a silent glottal stop). This explains why the Turkish politician, Tayyip Erdoğan, is too often referred to as Mr. *Er-dog-gone* rather than correctly as *Er-dough-on*. This being a book about Turkey, the diacritics will stay. Yet even I am not sufficiently pedantic to spell Istanbul as *İstanbul*, with a dotted capital *i*.

The use of Latin letters was never just a pedagogic tool. Nationalism depends on invented tradition, and in the case of the Turkish language we can see the cogwheels at work. The result was not simply to orientate Turkey toward the West but to blur cultural memory and cut the young republic off from its Ottoman roots. Turkish is the official language, according to the Constitution, and it is regarded as a key ingredient of the mortar that keeps the country unified. "Citizen, speak Turkish!" was an early nationalist injunction, and it wagged a finger at the wide use of Greek, French, and Armenian in commercial life. The conversion of Ottoman Turkish into Latinized Republican Turkish was accompanied by the wholesale purge of the Persian and Arabic vocabulary and its replacement with made-up words. Some of the neologisms produced by the Turkish Language Association (founded in 1931) are ingenious and self-explanatory. An American schoolchild untutored in ancient Greek might have to look up the word "synonymous," whereas their Turkish counterpart might intuit the sense of *eşanlamlı* ("with-equal-meaning"). Other expressions, like *özitirimligötürgeç* ("self-propelling-fetch-and-carry") for "automobile," never caught on. The transformation of the language was rapid. Those attending school now are not the first or even the second generation to have trouble understanding Atatürk's speeches, even in Latin alphabet transcription.

All Turkish nationals are obliged to send their children to Turkish-language primary school, though few believe their children can get on in the world with Turkish alone. Young teenagers take highly competitive exams to get into high schools taught in a foreign language (with certain subjects still taught in Turkish). Many universities are also taught via the medium of English. Yet if educated Turks happily speak foreign languages, many still balk at using the old Ottoman vocabulary, which they believe runs counter to Turkey's modernity project. Some writers resent having to use a stripped-down language impoverished by the lack of words common at the turn of the last century. However, they are aware they risk offending or, worse still, mystifying their readers.

Turkish also transcribes foreign words to make them look native. Turks take their car from the *garaj* to the *sinema*. But the first McDonald's sign appeared in Istanbul in 1986, and commercial centers and malls have become littered with international brand names spelled in a very un-Turkish way. The challenge of deciphering transcribed foreign words—for example, *komilfo* for *comme il faut*—is a disappearing pleasure. Turkish retail chains, too, favor un-Turkish brand names that travel across frontiers, like the clothing store Network or the cell-phone operator Turkcell. They learned their lesson from the first appliance firm, Arçelik (pronounced *ar-cheh-leek* rather than the rude way a non-Turk might assume), which is sensibly marketed abroad as Beko.

The Turkish Language Association is on the whole less obsessive than the Académie française in trying to protect the language from foreign influence. In a postmodern world and in contrast to the old die-hard insistence on linguistic purity, even Ottoman words are creeping back into commercial language. Just as Turkish-language films now hold their own in commercial competition in cinemas alongside rivals from Hollywood, and the Turkish *simit* (a sort of bagel) has made the transition from street food to fast food, so too Turkish is reappearing in logos and brand names. An example of this is Cola Turka—a parody of the trademark and a play on the Italianate word *alaturka*, which means "doing things the Turkish way." It is not an aggressively anti-American cola (as with Zam Zam Cola in Iran). It was launched with an advertising campaign starring Chevy Chase as a befuddled New Yorker who cannot understand why he suddenly grows a moustache, and everyone else around him adopts the stereotypes of Turkish life (even the hot dog stand switches over to selling chickpeas and rice) after a single sip.

In Ottoman times, French was the language of the foreign ministry because it was the language of the telegraph. Today the challenge is the Internet. Who can get by in business with an email address that has letters that don't exist on a QWERTY keyboard? Turks face an immediate difficulty. One prestigious Turkish university actually decided to omit the diacritics from its official name so it would not be ignored by search engines compiling citation indexes. A Turkish comic novel called *The Saint of Incipient Insanities* (2004) has among its characters Turkish students in Boston who face the loss of identity along with their diacritics. It is a dilemma the author, Elif Safak (or is it Shafak or Şafak?), knows only too well.

What are the regions of Turkey?

Turks are bemused by foreigners who think that because the country borders the Middle East, it ought to be covered in sand dunes. The Iraqi-Turkish frontier (219 miles in length) consists of high mountains and in winter is covered in snow. That border is a thousand miles away from Istanbul, an inland journey of great contrasts across rolling hills, high peaks, barren plateaus, and fertile basins. Turkey occupies a landmass slightly larger than Texas (783,632 square kilometers, just over 300,000 square miles) and is over three times the size of the United Kingdom. In terms of the variety of terrain and particularly the diversity of its plant life, however, Turkey exhibits the characteristics of a small continent. There are, for example, some 10,000 plant species (compared to some 13,000 in Europe), one in three of which is endemic to Turkey. Indeed there are more species in Istanbul province (2,000) than in the whole of the United Kingdom. While many know of Turkey's rich archaeological heritage, it possesses an equally valuable array of ecosystems—peat bogs, heath lands, steppes, coastal plains. Turkey possesses much forest (about a quarter of the land) but, as importantly, some half of the country is seminatural landscape, that is, not entirely remodeled by man. Many habitats are endangered by urbanization, mass tourism, and the mania of the State Hydraulic Works to build a dam wherever they see running water. However, Turkey is still a place to look out for birds and butterflies, snakes, and 500 species of bulbous plants.

Unseen beneath the earth are two major earthquake belts. The North Anatolian Fault runs east to west virtually the length of the country at a latitude that is immediately south of Istanbul. At its easternmost point, near the city of Erzurum, it is joined by the East Anatolian Fault, which runs at an angle down to the Gulf of Iskenderun near the Syrian border. Earthquake preparedness in Turkey is a must.

There are three general landscapes. There is the Mediterranean coastal system that extends in the west up the Aegean coast to the Sea of Marmara, just short of Istanbul. Istanbul is known as the meeting point of Europe and Asia but is also a junction with the Black Sea coastal system (and, by extension, Thrace), which resembles the temperate zones of continental Europe. Finally, there is the central Anatolian plateau and steppe leading eastward, to Iran.

Turkish geographers recognize seven regions, each with their own geography, culture, voting patterns, and, of course, cuisine:

1. *The Marmara Basin*, which has Istanbul at its center and includes European Turkey (bordered by Greece and Bulgaria) as well as the Asian side of the Dardanelles, and includes several important cities—Bursa, Izmit, Adapazarı, and Eskişehir.

2. *The Aegean Coast and its hinterland,* a prosperous agri-cultural area that looks toward the major west coast city of Izmir.

3. *The Mediterranean Coast,* a tourism strip rich in classical archaeological remains that is bounded to the north by the Taurus mountain range.

4. *Central Anatolia,* the conservative heartland with the major cities of Kayseri and Konya as well the capital Ankara.

5. *The Black Sea Coastal Region,* a land of corn, tea, hazel-nuts, and fresh anchovies that contains some of Turkey's most dramatic mountain scenery

6. *Eastern Anatolia,* the poorest part of the country (bordered by Iran and Armenia) that is largely Kurdish.

7. *Southeastern Anatolia,* a region bordering Syria and Iraq and dissected by both the Tigris and Euphrates rivers. It contains Diyarbakir, the unofficial Kurdish capital of Turkey, as well as the prosperous cities of Urfa (with a substantial Arab population) and Gaziantep.

An even simpler model than this school geography classifi-cation is the dichotomy of coastal cities and Anatolian heart-land, the former more cosmopolitan and outward looking, the latter more religious and conservative. This mirrors the contrast often made between the liberal seaboards of the United States and conservative Middle America, and it is just as dangerous a simplification.

2
HISTORICAL BACKGROUND

Who were the Ottomans and what is their relation to modern Turkey?

Today's Turkish Republic was previously part of an empire ruled over by the Ottoman dynasty. The word "Ottoman" is a Latin transcription of the Arabic for Osman I, the reputed founder of the dynasty. He fought his way into the attention of the Byzantine Greek historian George Pachymeres after defeating a Byzantine force in 1301 near modern Yalova, across the Marmara Sea from Istanbul. One puzzle of early Ottoman history is just how Osman and his heirs managed to establish supremacy over rival Muslim statelets to become the key power to oppose Byzantium. The Ottoman chroniclers, writing well after the fact, cultivate a picture of the early leaders as frontier warriors inspired by a sense of Islamic holy war. By their account, Osman was a *gazi*, the equivalent of a crusader knight, a title that was to be awarded to Mustafa Kemal Atatürk who deposed Osman's descendants some six centuries later. However, the notion of a fourteenth-century clash of civilizations is less favored by historians writing today, who see the Ottomans as consolidating power not just with the sword but also through strategic alliances and marriages—including with prominent Byzantine families—and in that sense harvesting divisions among rivals. Even so, the notion of Turkic tribes being pitted against Christendom survives in old Turkish films, which portray the borderlands as a cowboys-and-Indians battle of implacable foes—although in this case the Indians were noble and heroic, the cowboys corrupt and decadent.

By the time of the Ottoman ascendancy, Byzantium had long lost much direct control over Anatolia. The great defeat came in 1071 at the hands of the Seljuks, a Persianized Turkic dynasty, who had converted to Islam in the ninth century. The Battle of Malagzirt (at what is now the Turkish side of the Iranian border near Lake Van) opened the way to Muslim-Turkic colonization, which at one stage reached as far west as ancient Nicaea (Iznik). The Anatolia into which they moved was ethnically and culturally mixed, "with long-established Kurdish, Arab, Greek, Armenian and Jewish populations. ... Byzantium lay to the west, and in Cilicia and northern Syria were the Armenian and Crusader states, bordered to the south by the Muslim Mamluk state with its capital at Cairo."[1] The Seljuks were themselves defeated by the Mongols in 1243, opening the way to greater political disequilibrium in Anatolia of which the Ottomans ultimately were to take advantage.

The Turkish film industry is not alone in romanticizing Ottoman origins. Sultan Mehmet II saw himself as part of a classical pantheon, which included Alexander and the heroes of the *Iliad*, when at the age of twenty-one he successfully laid siege to Constantinople and, to his mind, avenged the defeat of Troy. The conquest of Constantinople in 1453 and its renaissance as "Istanbul" (although the name did not become official until a republican Municipal Act of

1930) is an event that is the "1066," "1492," and "1776" of Ottoman history—1453 is a date every schoolchild knows. It is mourned by Greeks as the end of Byzantium and observed in Turkey as the coming of age of Ottoman imperial power. Indeed, May 29, the day the Ottomans breached the city wall, is (depending on the party in power) celebrated with historical reenactments and public parades. For many new Turkish migrants to the city, the conquest of an alien, cosmopolitan city has particular resonance.

Istanbul became the principal seat of the dynasty (there were earlier capitals in Bursa and Edirne), and the urban aesthetic that developed—the cultivation of the tulip and the arabesque, the fusion of dome and minaret, and the merging of Byzantine and Islamic court traditions—are what most people associate with high Ottoman culture. However, the Ottoman Empire was well established before the siege. The Constantinople of 1453 was already a pale shadow of its imperial past, never having recovered from being looted in 1204 by the Latin army of the Fourth Crusade. Byzantium had already been reduced to a city-state within an Ottoman sea that included much of today's Greece and Bulgaria and extended from Niš in Serbia to Western Anatolia.

By the mid-sixteenth century the Ottoman domains stretched further, from Hungary to the Arabian Peninsula, and from North Africa to the Caucasus. Another misconception about the Ottoman Empire is that it was a polity fueled by the spoils of westward conquest and that once the military achieved its full reach, the empire spun inexorably into decline. The empire's ability to wage war depended on rural prosperity, efficient taxation, and a sophisticated system of administration. In practice, the sultan's armies fought equally hard campaigns against Iranian foes in the East. Baghdad, was captured, lost, and recaptured from the Safavids between 1534 and 1638. The Ottomans faced opposition as well from rival Muslim emirates within their own backyard. The conquest by Selim I (r. 1512–1520) of the Islamic heartlands—of Damascus and Cairo as well as Mecca and Medina—allowed the Ottoman throne to annex the title of "caliph," the spiritual leader of the Islamic world. It is common to think of the reign of Süleyman (r. 1520–1566) as the apogee of the classical age. In English he is known as the "Magnificent" but in Turkish he is "The Law Maker," emphasizing the institutionalization of power that took place in his time. And if the empire did decline after the failed second siege of Vienna in 1683, it took nearly two and a half centuries to hit the bottom.

The Ottomans referred to their realm as a "state" ruled by the sultan and did not use the word "empire." Theirs was one contiguous territory rather than a mother country with overseas colonies. Even so, it is fair to say that many Turks would be surprised to be confronted with the suggestion that they are heirs to a colonial power. The Republican Turks at first disparaged their own sultanic past, but this was nothing compared to the national histories of the Balkans and the Middle East that vilified the "Ottoman night" from which they emerged in the early nineteenth century. However, just as modern Turkey has learned to take pride in its Ottoman past, scholars elsewhere have been (slowly) revising the narrative of their own past, or at least looking beyond the turbulent prologue to World War I in which the character of the empire changed dramatically. Part of the Ottoman legacy was a policy of official toleration (a concept of acceptance rather than of equality) of other faiths. This has led some today to refer nostalgically to a golden age or *pax Ottomanica with pa Ottomanica* in regions now troubled by ethnic tensions. Others refer to recent Turkish governments' efforts to exert cultural or economic influence over its "near abroad" and become a regional power as a form of neo-Ottomanism. While this is not a policy to which any politician would openly subscribe, the Ottoman past does provide a precedent for the more relaxed acceptance of overlapping identities as well as an openness to both East and West. Indeed, as the empire disintegrated during the nineteenth and early twentieth centuries, great waves of refugees came to what is now Turkey and formed a Balkan or Caucasian diaspora. Many of the most fervent Turkish nationalists of the 1920s and 1930s, or the most ardent anti-Communists of the 1960s, either were themselves displaced by conflict as the empire shrank or were descendants of those who were displaced.

By a similar token, Turkey was never colonized by the great powers (though parts were occupied very briefly after 1918), which distinguishes it from most other twentieth-century developing nations. What the implications of this are for the country's current political culture are the subject of debate, but they may help account for a determination to engage with the project of Westernization. Turkey—unlike India or Venezuela—is not in a love-hate relationship with a "mother" culture but in a dialogue with its own past, and between itself and the outside world.[2]

The Ottomans in the nineteenth century were painfully aware of their declining power as they faced ethnicity-based civil rebellions allied to their imperial rivals. The Tanzimat, a reform program declared in 1839, marks a conscious effort to "catch up" with the West, but the program could not help but be compromised as the empire became hopelessly mired in debt. The Ottoman Public Debt Administration established in 1881 was essentially a creditors union (far more onerous than any IMF standby agreement) by which foreign bankers took control of the public purse. Equally resented were the famed "capitulations," that is, commercial and trading concessions demanded by Western powers and enjoyed by foreign nationals and those non-Muslim adopting a foreign nationality. The generation that founded the new republic was determined to beat Europe at its own game. The Ottoman Empire ended with the abolition of the sultanate in 1922. The religious office of the caliphate was abolished two years later.

In September 2009, a coffin was carried from the courtyard of Istanbul's Blue Mosque to an imperial mausoleum, where it was laid next to that of Sultan Abdülhamid II. In it was Osman Ertuğrul, born in 1912, the last of his line to have been raised at court and dangled on a reigning sultan's knee. The grandson of Abdülhamid II, he spent most of his life in exile, latterly in a rent-controlled apartment in New York, and was only allowed to return to Turkey in 1992, when he toured Dolmabahçe Palace, his childhood home, as just another member of a guided tour. His funeral, although not an official state event, was attended by government ministers—a quiet indication that modern Turkey has come to terms with the empire it succeeded.

What was the genesis of modern Turkey?

On the eve of World War I, the Ottoman Empire was teetering on financial ruin and institutional collapse. It lost virtual control over North Africa and most of its European territory, and it grappled to contain civil unrest in Yemen and even parts of Anatolia. The Young Turk revolution in 1908, intended to create a constitutional monarchy, instead resulted in the sultan becoming a figurehead for a military junta. By 1913 the empire's fortunes lay in the hands of Enver Pasha—a military officer who had married into the royal family. He could no longer work Abdülhamid's strategy of playing adversaries against each other. Partly through bad judgment and partly through bad British diplomacy, he maneuvered into an alliance with the German-led Central Powers as the best way of defending the empire's remaining territory. In a sense, that defense began with the Balkan Wars (1912–1913) and only ended with the declaration of the Republic in 1923, one decade later.

The immediate price of the Ottoman Empire's defeat in World War I was the Treaty of Sèvres (1920). This envisaged the dismemberment of the empire; the establishment of Armenian and Kurdish states in the east; the de facto occupation of Istanbul; and the division of much of the Aegean and Mediterranean coasts into zones of influence controlled by the victorious Triple Entente of France, Britain, and Italy, together with Greece. A rebel nationalist movement garrisoned in Ankara that defended Turkey's integrity as a new nation-state defied not just the Entente Powers but also the sultan in occupied Istanbul. The Turkish War of Liberation refers to a four-year period beginning in 1919, during which the remnants of the Ottoman army and newly recruited irregulars set out to prove Sèvres unenforceable. The principal battles were fought between 1921 and 1922 against a Greek force that tried, with Britain's initial encouragement, to extend their occupation of the city of Izmir further inland. The eventual routing of the Greek army and the lack of will of a war-weary Europe to enforce an occupation resulted in a new agreement, the Treaty of Lausanne, which in 1923 recognized the Turkey of today.

They say that generals are forever fighting their last war, and the same might apply to nations. It wasn't all that long ago that the clash of civilizations in European minds referred to the fight against fascism. The "axis of evil" was literally the Axis Powers that strove to impose a racist form of totalitarianism on the rest of the continent. The need to bury the fascist legacy of World War II and impose a permanent peace based on the common interests of Germany and France is very much at the heart of today's unified Europe. Turkey sat out that conflict, remaining neutral until January 1945.

Turkey's own harrowing memory, enshrined in national holidays and school history books, is the aftermath of World War I. That war, and the invasion and civil war that followed, cost the lives of some 20 percent of the population and devastated land, livestock, and entire cities.[3] The real battles the country then fought for national sovereignty continue to be reenacted at various levels. It is only a mild exaggeration to paint Turkey as in a state of constant vigilance against real and imagined attempts by the outside world to reinstate the Treaty of Sèvres. Rhetorical battles with an Armenian diaspora, the real skirmishes with Kurdish separatists, an obsession with the fate of the oil-rich northern Iraqi city of Kirkuk, and past tensions with Greece in the Aegean and over Cyprus in the Mediterranean—these are all legacies of confrontations that the rest of Europe has largely forgotten.

Turks themselves sometimes refer to their "young republic" as an explanation for why public institutions are inchoate or still operate in low gear. Yet the present state was founded long enough in the past—it will soon be a century—that by any reckoning it should have outgrown juvenilia. The Turkish Republic has changed its shape in the intervening years; the initial constitution was replaced twice (1961,

1982), coinciding with two of three direct military coups (1960, 1971, and 1980). As of this writing, there are efforts to change it a third time. Yet Turkey celebrates its national day on October 29, the date in 1923 when the Republic was first declared. From that perspective, it has older institutions than the majority of European nations, which did not assume their current shape until the end of World War II or following the fall of the Soviet Empire.

Who was Atatürk and why is his picture everywhere?

It doesn't take long for the most casual visitor to conclude that Turkey ascribes to the "great man" view of history. Portraits of Mustafa Kemal Atatürk (1881–1938) hang in schools, public offices, private businesses, and many homes. In a sense, Atatürk is a combination of George Washington Winston Churchill, and Franklin Delano Roosevelt, and he is celebrated as both soldier and statesman. At the end of World War I, when the Ottoman Empire was being carved into Allied spheres of influence and even Istanbul was under occupation, Atatürk led a movement of national resistance. The forces under his command reclaimed virtually all the territory that constitutes today's modern Republic.[4]

Atatürk was chosen president by the National Assembly, a post he held until his death in 1938. His second and in many ways more dramatic accomplishment was as a political leader who gave the new state a determinedly modern orientation. The Turkish Republic set out to impose its authority over the remnants of the old regime. The capital was moved from Istanbul to Ankara, located 220 miles (350 kilometers) to the west, away from the sway of imperial decadence and reactionary clerics, and out of the reach of European powers.

Atatürk lent his name to a series of reforms that he defined as nothing short of a series of revolutions. Making men wear a Western-style brimmed hat instead of the fez, or altering the calendar to make Saturday and Sunday the weekend, might not seem radical or subversive, but a cumulative weight of change led to genuine transformation in the most intimate moments of peoples' lives. Women were encouraged to enter more fully into public life—and in order to do so, they unveiled. In a benign sort of Orwellian exercise, even the words in people's heads began to change. The adoption of the Latin alphabet proved an even more powerful fulcrum for tilting the new Republic toward the West.

Common sense suggests Atatürk neither won wars single-handedly nor modernized the country on his own. Many of those who worked shoulder-to-shoulder with him saw their reputations overshadowed. There is little doubt that he ruled dictatorially. While there was no Stalinist-like reign of terror, there were purges and some opposition figures were hanged. In 1937 a rebellion in the Kurdish province of Dersim (now Tunceli) was brutally suppressed. Arguably, some of the Atatürkist "revolutions," even the emancipation of women, were codifications of transformations already in the air. World War I, in the Ottoman Empire no less than in the rest of Europe, tore at the old order and was an accelerator of social change. Arguably, too, Atatürk's fifteen years as autocratic head of state set an unwieldy precedent for the postwar period, when Turkey embarked on multiparty democracy. Modernization by fiat was bound to provoke a backlash after Atatürk's death. Such arguments are heard, but not often. One of his reforms was the adoption of Western-style surnames. His own means "Father of the Turks," and modern Turkey is happy to bask in that paternalism. Most regard his person as inspirational. The nation still stands to silent attention on the morning of every November 10 to mark the moment of his death.

What is Atatürk's legacy?

Atatürk was essentially a pragmatist, and though his founding vision is enshrined as inviolable in the very first sentence of the constitution, it is not clear in every instance how his legacy applies today. That does not stop those in authority from speaking in his name.

The political party he founded, the Republican People's Party, was dedicated to six "arrows" or founding principles; some of these are self-explanatory or rhetorical (a commitment to a republican form of government, to Turkey as a nation-state, and to a belief that sovereignty derives from the people). Others have become less clear over time, such as whether Turkey is a secular state in the sense of relegating religion to the individual conscience or in the Jacobin sense of keeping it firmly under an official thumb. A fifth principle, enshrining the role of the state in the economy, made sense during the 1920s and 1930s when there was no investment to kick-start development and when memories were still fresh of the debt regime imposed by foreign bankers over Ottoman administration. "Etatism" is not, however, a philosophy that passes muster with the IMF, to whom Turkey appealed for help throughout the 1990s to control what had become a bloated state sector. Equally problematic is a belief in revolution. At the time of its formulation it meant endorsement of the unflinching character of Atatürk's reforms in the face of conservative opposition. Its antonym is "reactionary" or "backwardness" (*irtica* in Turkish), the mindset of those who would undermine Republican virtues, usually in the name of religion. In time, however, loyalty to the Atatürk revolution became the marching song of an officer class and its bureaucratic allies, both of which were determined to protect the people from their own politicians.

Democracy was notably not one of the founding six arrows. Atatürk was a member of a revolutionary cadre. His "Address to Turkish youth" of 1927 warns against those who, although holding high office, may be "in error," even "traitors," or who were "in league with the country's invaders." This was clearly a reference to the post–World War I Allied occupation and the toppling of the monarchy. However, Atatürk's example as purveyor of permanent revolution was to legitimate military intervention in civilian rule.

Turks draw a distinction between respect for the historical person of Atatürk and *Kemalism*, a term often used pejoratively to describe those who would evoke his authority to support their own interests. Yet most schoolbooks closely identify Atatürk's life with that of the nation. He is often spoken of as being "immortal," living on eternally in his compatriots' hearts. His escape in 1919 from Allied-occupied Istanbul to the Black Sea town of Samsun to initiate a national resistance is celebrated with the Soviet-sounding "Youth and Sports Day." Though a Kemalist would blanch at the comparison, it has acquired the same sort of symbolic resonance as the Prophet Mohammed's flight to Medina.

If there is a cult of Atatürk, it is subject to fashion and its high priests are not always those one might expect. In 1950, twelve years after his death, the party Atatürk founded—the Republican People's Party—was voted out of office, and his political successor and military second-in-command, İsmet İnönü, was dispatched into opposition. The party that replaced them, the Democrat Party, was itself ousted by the military, in effect for betraying the revolution. Yet while in power the Democrat Party was more Atatürkist than Atatürk himself in its attempt to seize İnönü's mantle of legitimacy. Law number 5816, which makes insulting Atatürk's memory an offense punishable by up to three years in jail, dates from 1951. The Justice and Development (AK) Party, which formed a government for the first time in 2002, has been accused by Turkish secularists of trampling on Atatürk's grave, yet it too has kept on the statute books laws under which access to YouTube was blocked for over two years, ostensibly because the site housed unflattering postings about the national hero.

It would be wrong to suggest there has been no revision of Mustafa Kemal's place in Turkish history. A recent biography of Latife, whom he married in 1923 and divorced two-and-a-half years later, was well received, as was a docudrama showing him to have a more human side. Even so, both works provoked nuisance prosecutions under Law 1518. The possibility of Atatürk suffering Lenin's fate and being knocked off the pedestal atop which Turkish officialdom has labored to place him seems remote. Different factions fight to appropriate his legacy; to discredit it would be the equivalent of saying Turkey should not exist.

Atatürk represents a common denominator about what modern Turkey is all about. First is the creation of a nation within secure boundaries, one that embraces modernity, that keeps religion largely confined to the private realm, and that takes its international responsibilities seriously. High in the pantheon of most-quoted sayings is "peace at home, peace abroad," which translates as "let's behave ourselves and not go around looking for trouble"; it is not a bad motto, if not always easy to keep to. Often the key to a person's attitude toward Atatürk is the picture they hang of him on the wall—the soldier alone before the battle or the urbane president hobnobbing with Edward VIII. An austere death mask shows an attitude of unreconstructed devotion. I recall the picture in the office of a confectionery tycoon who had a reputation for leaning toward the religious right. His Atatürk icon was a rare photo of a shy man, no longer young, his face partly obscured as he handed out sweets to children.

Are there any Atatürk jokes (and, if so, does anyone laugh at them)?

Not many, which might seem odd because Turks have a tradition of political caricature. One of the most famous humor magazines (*Akbaba*, or "vulture") began life in 1922. It's hard to think of another politician who has escaped the satirist's pen. Turkish political humor goes back as least as far as Nasreddin Hodja, the famous Anatolian fool, who bad-mouthed the all-powerful Tamerlane (1336–1405) to a perfect stranger: "Do you know who I am?" the stranger asked, and when the Hodja shook his head "no," the man replied, "I am Tamerlane!" "Ah! But do you know who I am?" the Hodja asked, and when Tamerlane shook his head "no," the Hodja replied, "Good!" and ran for the hills.

There is a similar story about Atatürk, more anecdote than joke, and I include it despite its violation of this book's title to include only things on a need-to-know basis. In this case, the Hodja was a waiter collecting orders for Turkish coffee. One night, the waiter walked the length of an enormous table—at which sat Mustafa Kemal—listening to each guest's involved preference for this or that much sugar, or no sugar at all, yet he never bothered to write anything down. Eventually, he reappeared and handed out the cups. Mustafa Kemal sipped his coffee and, to his amazement, it was just the way he had requested. "How on earth did you manage to get the orders straight?" he asked the waiter. "I remembered yours," the waiter replied. "Who cares about the rest?"

A necessary addendum is that Turkish politicians are not very good at laughing at themselves. As prime minister, Tayyip Erdoğan, leader of the Justice and Development Party, actually sued a caricaturist who depicted him as a cat tangled up in a ball of wool. Then again, the symbol of Erdoğan's party is an old-fashioned, environmentally hostile, incandescent light bulb, and there are no jokes about how many people it would take to change this.

Where does Turkey fit into world history?

Scratch the earth in Turkey and you find traces of antiquity; lay a tunnel for a subway system in Istanbul and you uncover a Byzantine harbor, silted over for the last 900 years. In 2005 construction for a new subway stop was suspended after excavations uncovered a flotilla of thirty-two sunken ships— large galleys, cargo ships, and small lighters used to offload freight—embalmed in the sand. The finds, dating from the seventh to the eleventh centuries, have been described as the current generation's discovery of the Pyramids and one that will force scholars to rethink life and trade in the Mediterranean and Medieval Europe. The boats themselves, able to withstand enormous forces of nature, represent the most highly engineered structures of their age, as cutting-edge in their way as the Japanese design of the earthquake-proof tunnel semi-submerged on the sea floor that led to their discovery. Those excavations also uncovered a ritual burial site some 8,000 years old, which at a stroke gives Istanbul a late Neolithic past.

Turkey is by no means a land time forgot. The land mass it occupies has been at the center of much human history. To the east are the headwaters of the Tigris and the Euphrates, the two rivers that define ancient Mesopotamia and the reputed cradle of civilization. To the west are the straits separating Europe from Asia—from Bronze Age Troy through the Gallipoli campaigns of World War I, all the way to the end of the Cold War, the Dardanelles have been a crucial defensive pinch point. Harran, the birthplace of Abraham, is inside Turkey's southern border with Syria. Saint Paul was "of" Tarsus, today a bustling Mediterranean city with a quarter of a million people. It is also where in 41 B.C. Anthony first set eyes on Cleopatra, and where the armies of Alexander the Great descended from the Anatolian plateau to the coast. In central Turkey, amid fields planted with hops, is Çatalhöyük, which in 7400 B.C. was home to a community of 5,000 people, qualifying it as one of the first cities on earth (and proof, if it were needed, of the close link between civilization and the brewing of beer). Turkey is littered with the great Bronze and Iron Age fortresses built by the Hittites and Urartians; classical Greek and Roman theaters and temples; and the monastic communities of the early Church. And this is all before the eleventh century, when Turks made their way west and Anatolia became a "New World" for the Islamic world just as America was to become for Christendom. The Great Mosque of Divriği is an extravagant hybrid structure, the product of a Gaudi-like imagination, built in a minor Seljuk beylik in eastern Anatolia in 1299. The skyline of Istanbul is dominated by the Byzantine Cathedral of Hagia Sofia

(A.D. 537) and the Ottoman Sultan Ahmed (or Blue) Mosque (A.D. 1616), which attests to its importance as the capital of two great empires and the center of two world religions for over 1,500 years.

How seriously does Turkey take its obligation to preserve the past?

On one hand, very seriously. There is a whole raft of legislation to protect historical properties, control and protect the restoration of historical buildings and neighborhoods, and prevent antiquities being taken abroad. The Istanbul Archaeological Museum, founded in 1891 by statesman-painter-archaeologist Osman Hamdi Bey, played a seminal role in the formulation of state policy toward art and antiquities as well as instilled a tradition of museum curatorship. There are many fine regional museums and well-kept archaeological sites. Ankara's Museum of Anatolian Civilizations is world-class. Cultural heritage management is attracting more and more dedicated young people, and new generations of archaeologists and restorers have the chance to learn their craft on the spot, with the benefit of extraordinarily significant sites and artifacts close at hand.

Turkey has a financial incentive to get it right. The country has entered the ranks of the world's top ten tourism destinations (according to the World Tourism Organization), targeting some 30 million foreign visitors (in 2011) in an industry currently worth $21 billion. Well over 20 million people (not just foreigners, of course) visit museums and sites maintained by the Ministry of Culture and Tourism every year. Hagia Sofia, Topkapı Palace, and the Mevlana Museum in Konya are the three most visited museums.

Ephesus, Cappadocia, and the calcified cliffs and thermal springs of Hierapolis (Pamukkale) are the most visited ruins. If Turkey is learning to value the past, it is in part because the past has real financial value.

On the other hand, that culture and tourism share a ministry (an arrangement not unique to Turkey) can mean that it is not always clear which is the mistress and which the handmaiden. The desire to convert sites into tour-bus-worthy attractions can take precedence over the need to learn from the past. Many still think of archaeology as a treasure hunt for great objects rather than an investigation that requires landscapes and context to be preserved. Then there are a score of problems imposed by the sheer volume of history to be preserved. The Istanbul Archaeological Museum is assigned to look after all the city's antiquities and this scope is beyond its resources. Regrettably, the revenue from (often expensive) admission tickets goes to the central treasury and not to the monuments and museums themselves. Preserving the past is not just a question of looking after objects but having the right legislation and supervisory structures. Protecting known sites is easier than anticipating where the bulldozers will go next. Archaeologists, dependent on ministerial goodwill for their permits, are often reluctant to join the public debate. A few examples will hint at the problems.

As with the subway excavations cited above, archaeologists and scholars often only become aware of important finds when they are imperiled. The Byzantine harbor was buried under apartment buildings that had been built after the 1950s on what had once been an inner-city market garden. Remarkably, the subway was delayed several years to allow for the emergency excavations to be held. This was not the case on the Euphrates River where, in 2000, archaeologists were powerless to stop the rising level of the reservoir of the newly constructed Birecik Dam. This resulted in a race against time to rescue a stunning series of floor mosaics from the late Roman frontier city of Zeugma. Some of these are now safely in a purpose-built museum in the nearby city of Gaziantep, while those on high ground are preserved on site. Other treasures, however, are now submerged. And while it was the mosaics that grabbed the attention of the world's media, it was the Roman fortress itself that caught the imagination of historians—and that now may never be found.

In the late 1980s the mayor of Istanbul cleared the shores of Istanbul's Golden Horn and installed a much-needed sewage system. Less praiseworthy, not a single shard was recovered in what must surely have been one of the most important archaeological sites in the city. What Byzantine "monuments of unageing intellect" might have been lost in the construction no one can know. Economic pressures to develop urban land and coastlines, or even just to build highways, also hint at undocumented destruction. In past decades, highways ripped through prehistoric mounds as large as Troy between Istanbul and Edirne.

Many of the country's most important digs race against the clock to rescue major sites while an army of bulldozers waits, engines running. Even so, work on the Byzantine harbor, mentioned above, continued for seven years although heavy construction on the project continued at the same time. There are clear indications that this delay, along with the prospect of other undertakings in the pipeline being held up, has caused government patience to wear thin. Prime Minister Erdoğan, in a speech in February 2011, expressed his annoyance with "bits of old pot" that were getting in the way of major infrastructure projects. "People have to first," he said, while announcing the creation of a virtually new city on Istanbul's remaining green belt along the Black Sea, with a new Bosphorus bridge as well as a Panama-style canal that would cut the Thracian Peninsula in two.

New legislation removes responsibility for designating sites as being of historical importance away from the Ministry of Culture and Tourism. Instead protection is now the responsibility of the Ministry for the Environment, which has a poor reputation for standing up against wholesale development. So while time may be its subject matter, time is not a luxury Turkish archaeology enjoys.

Many complain about the "Disneyfication" of Istanbul's monumental Theodosian-era land walls, which were not so much restored as prettified (do you rebuild the wall to what it looked like in the fifth century, or the tenth, or the nineteenth?) and, many suspect, made more vulnerable to earthquake. As if that were not bad enough, in 2009 an ancient community of Romani that can be traced back to the fifteenth century—featured in the old James Bond film, *From Russia with Love*—was forcibly evicted from their homes in the Sulukule neighborhood beside the land walls. They were given scant compensation to make way for a faux-Ottoman-looking housing development, a shopping center, and a hotel. Many wonder why the historical peninsula of Istanbul has not been converted into an archaeological park like that of Rome. Indeed, there is not even an official inventory of historical sites and monuments; Turkey reneged on its commitment to UNESCO to produce a master plan for the management of historical properties by 2009. The historical peninsula lives with the constant threat of being struck off the UNESCO list of World Heritage Sites—the equivalent of being told that Istanbul is not capable of looking after its history. UNESCO objects to the city's failure to assess the impact of a proposed underwater tunnel to the Asian side of the city and thus pump traffic into the historical peninsula. In its battle with Mammon and urban developers, culture often fights with one hand behind its back.

The conservation of buildings and of historical areas is the subject of considerable academic controversy. The fantastical stonework on the façade of the mosque at Divriği is genuinely in peril, but arguments rage about whether the whole building should be dismantled and moved, put under a glass structure, or simply patched up piecemeal against the weathering of centuries. Each solution creates its own problems. In Istanbul, the church of Saints Sergius and Bacchus is a building of stunning innovation built by Emperor Justinian in 527 and converted by the Ottomans into a mosque—Küçük Ayasofya Camii, or the Small Haghia Sophia Mosque—nearly 1,000 years later under the patronage of Sultan Bayezid II's Chief White Eunuch, Hüseyin Ağa. In 2005 it underwent much-needed conservation work to protect it against earthquakes and vibrations from nearby train tracks. This would have allowed for academic investigation to unlock the edifice's secrets. Instead, the work was done by a local contractor in virtual secrecy and the opportunity was lost. A structure that should have been treated like a rare manuscript was treated like an apartment building with a leaky roof.

In 1935 Turkey came up with a "King Solomon's baby" solution for what is probably Istanbul's most important monument, Haghia Sophia. Built as a Byzantine cathedral, it was transformed into a mosque after 1453 and claimed by both faiths. The solution was to turn it into a museum. This and the subsequent restoration of the mosaic panels, which was begun in cooperation with the Byzantine Institute of

America in the 1940s, would suggest that Turkish cultural policy is far from insular.

Scores of non-Turkish universities are engaged in the excavation of the most important sites in the country—archaeologists from the universities of Cincinnati and Tübingen work in Troy, while at the Bronze Age site of Çatalhöyük Turkish archaeologists from the local Selçuk University work with a long list of collaborators from Stanford University, the British Institute at Ankara, University of California at Berkeley, and London University.

Antiquities are antiquities and, no matter their provenance, they are protected by the same laws. Of course it would be foolish to pretend that nationalism and ideology play no role in cultural policy. Increasingly, Turkish archaeologists have claimed priority for the right to excavate at sites. Sites and monuments that figure in "official" Turkish history are better looked after than those that do not. The Seljuk mosque in the medieval city of Ani, for example, was restored while nearby Armenian churches had been allowed to deteriorate. However, attitudes are changing and the Cultural Ministry is now committed to restoring the churches as well. The sea change occurred with the restoration of the tenth-century Armenian cathedral church on Akhtamar (or Akdamar) island in Lake Van near the Iranian border, presented at the time as an example of Turkey's embrace of multiculturalism. Archeologists working in Turkey find fault not so much with ideological obstacles as government tender procedures that result in excavations and restorations going to the lowest bidder rather than the most capable or scholarly.

At the same time, Turkey is in an uneasy relation with its Byzantine past. That past is far too omnipresent to ignore, given the prominence of Aya Sofia on the Istanbul skyline. Though Istanbul often boasts of having been, uniquely, the capital of two empires and the center of two major world religions, the city authorities often are reluctant to celebrate the first. These attitudes have been changing, particularly given the political rapprochement with Greece that began in 1999. In 2010, as part of the European Capital of Culture festivities, Istanbul's Sabanci Museum staged "From Byzantion to Istanbul: 8000 Years of a Capital," which drew favorable comparisons to similar blockbusters in New York's Metropolitan Museum or London's Royal Academy. Even so, it is still the exception to see even the word "Byzantium" in official publications, and school curricula similarly gloss over the period.

If official attitudes toward monuments reflect nationalist sentiment, then the content of that nationalism has itself changed. In the 1920s and 1930s, the founders of the Republic were anxious to ignore not just Byzantium but the Ottoman legacy as well. They took enormous interest in the pre-antiquity of Anatolia—particularly the late Bronze Age Hittite civilization whose discovery in the late nineteenth century corresponded to their own days as students. Wanting to trace their own origins to "native" Anatolian, pre-Islamic, peoples is not dissimilar to Egyptians identifying with the pharaonic past.

After 1980, however, it became far more acceptable to commemorate the Ottoman and Islamic past as authorities began to court popular sentiment. One of the great debates that raged in Ankara and in the courts was whether the religiously conservative city administrators could change its symbol from a Hittite-inspired sun to a more Islamic motif. In the end, the city settled on a value-neutral logo based on the Ankara cat, which has one eye blue and the other yellow. In 2010 Istanbul was designated a "European Capital of Culture" to promote its integration with the European Union. Much of the budget was used for the maintenance of historically important mosques.

3

ECONOMY

What is Turkey's economic potential ... ?

Turkey comfortably takes its place at G20 summits. It is, according to most reckonings of nominal GDP, the seventeenth largest economy in the world and the eight largest and fastest growing in Europe. Istanbul alone has a GDP greater than that of Hungary or the Czech Republic, or indeed greater than any of the post-2004 members of the European Union enlargement with the exception of Poland. Yet for all its brawn, Turkey has not yet earned a slot in the acronym coined by the gnomes at Goldman Sachs—BRIC—to describe those continent-sized nations (Brazil, Russia, India, China) to whom the future is reputed to belong. Instead, it is relegated to the "N11" (Next 11) as a newly industrialized country, or what the London-based indexing company FTSE calls an "advanced emerging economy." Turkey was badly affected by the international credit squeeze in 2008–2009, and particularly by the resulting contraction of its export markets. However, it was quick out of the gates the following year with a growth rate of 8.9 percent compared to OECD averages, which are closer to 2 percent. A country that had long suffered chronic structural problems was suddenly turning heads as one of the motors of European recovery. Turkey still struggles with some of its old demons, including the legacy of the dead weight of a large and politically driven state presence in the economy. However, its track record of fiscal discipline in recent years and competent economic management means that the golden apple—an "investment grade" status from the international rating agencies—is near enough to touch.

Turkey's quest for normalcy has been the result of a long and at times painful process of capital accumulation. Unlike its carbon-rich neighbors, Turkey has not been able to use the shortcut (or curse!) of one commodity. The resources it does possess—fertile land, fresh water, abundant sunshine, and more than its fair share of a chemical used in glass and ceramic production called "boron"—are ones for which there is no international spot market. When Turkish business goes on the road to sell the country abroad, the PowerPoint presentation inevitably bullet-points another, far less tangible resource—the country's great potential. Turkey is a young and populous nation in which average income has tripled over the last decade, hovering above the $10,000 per capita mark. Household liabilities as a proportion of GDP is modest—17.3 percent including credit card debt (as of 2010, according to Central Bank figures), compared to nearly 60 percent in the European Union or closer to the 100 percent range for the United States. This means that far from drowning in vats of toxic debt, Turkish consumers are just beginning to get their feet wet. Not surprisingly, insurance, healthcare, and other consumer-oriented sectors view Turkey as Europe's final frontier, just as Dutch and Dubai property developers jostle to find a bit of undeveloped urban land to build one more shopping mall. It is a country in the process of growing its own middle class.

Driving this is the one natural advantage to which Turkey does lay claim, which is, as the real estate mantra would have it, "location, location, location." That same Turkish road-show paints a picture of a complex economy in its own right, but one well situated to become a conduit of goods and services between Europe and the resource-rich nations of the Middle East and the former Soviet Union. Turkey possesses a sophisticated financial sector but also the entrepreneurial "street smarts" to make it an ideal launch pad for markets inaccessible to others but within its orbit. Turkish contractors, for example, may not be unique in building airports, highways, and luxury hotels, but they do so in Libya, Iraq, Sudan, and Turkmenistan.

The other side of the equation is that in 1996 Turkey entered into a full customs union with the European Union on manufactured goods. This means that Turkish industries compete with those in the most developed economies. It also means that firms invested in Turkey can utilize lower labor costs and free access to European markets. This has proved the impetus behind the growth of an electrical consumer goods sector (turn on a television set in Europe and chances are it was "Made in Turkey") as well as an automotive industry that includes trucks and buses. Industries such as glass or cement hedge their bets, producing for the growing domestic market but also for export. Turkey's large textile industry can never make a generic T-shirt as cheaply as factories in Bangladesh. However, it can meet delivery times and quality standards for a prêt-à-porter fashion item for a German department store and, in the process, attempt to develop its own brand names and retail chains abroad.

Industry, however, represents merely 28 percent of Turkey's GDP. Low as that figure might seem, it still makes

Turkey the industrial powerhouse of a region that includes Russia and Iran (if one excludes petroleum production). The service sector, including tourism, telecommunications, and finance, make up 62 percent. Agriculture makes up for the rest—a small percentage, perhaps, but still a major source of employment.

Despite having no significant hydrocarbons of its own, Turkey is attempting to establish itself as an energy corridor. It sits on the contemporary equivalent of the ancient trade route, carrying gas and oil from Iraq, Azerbaijan, Iran, Turkmenistan, and Russia. The Mediterranean port of Ceyhan, for example, is the terminus for the Baku-Tbilisi-Ceyhan (BTC) pipeline that carries crude some 1,100 miles from the Caspian Sea. Ceyhan is also the outlet for oil from Kirkuk, Iraq's most important oil export line. A further pipeline is proposed to run from Samsun on the Black Sea to Ceyhan. This would divert Black Sea oil-tanker trade away from Istanbul's narrow Bosphorus Straits, where nearly 52,000 vessels a year carry 100 million tons of oil and petroleum, posing an obvious risk to the megalopolis they traverse. The most significant pipeline—still in the "pipeline" stage of development—is Nabucco, which would bring Caspian and Middle East natural gas across Turkey to as far west as Austria. Nabucco is backed enthusiastically by the European Union as it would have the potential to relieve Europe's dependence on Russia. Buying gas from Iran against the wishes of Washington, challenging Moscow's control over the energy tap to Europe, and becoming involved in the Arab-Kurdish petropolitics of Iraq—all this is part of a new "great game" in which Turkey has become a player. It engages in this game willingly; energy experts point out that revenue from the carriage trade of gas and oil does not offset the cost of building the pipeline. However, economic and strategic power interests are hard to untangle.

... And Turkey's economic weaknesses?

Unsaturated markets and comparative labor costs are advantages that will see the country only as far as the medium term. Indeed, some Turkish firms have begun to move their operations to countries with even lower labor costs. While Europe fears the influx of Turkish labor, Turkey itself attracts, according to some estimates, up to a million illegal economic migrants. A youthful demographic means Turkey postpones the "pension trap" confronting most EU nations (where an aging population is dependent on an ever-shrinking workforce). The converse of this is that Turkey must provide opportunity for its young people. High rates of youth unemployment and a large, informal sector where workers have few benefits and security means that not everyone's view of the country's future is rose-tinted. Turkey, according to the United Nations Development Program (UNDP), punches below its economic weight in terms of the welfare of its own people. In the world, it ranks fifty-fourth in purchasing-power-parity-adjusted GDP per capita but eighty-third in the 2010 UNDP human development index, all of which suggests at some point the government will have to address the demand for better social services and—more urgently—a correction of the disparities between different parts of the country.

Despite countless incentive schemes to redress the balance, there are still profound inequalities between regions. Western Turkey and the Mediterranean coastal cities account for the lion's share of the country's economy—some 80 percent of value added. Eastern provinces account for less than 10 percent, with central Anatolia and the Black Sea making up the rest. Istanbul, the most productive part of the country, has a GDP twenty times that of its poor relation in the Northeast.[1] The situation of "two nations" in Turkey is an obvious source of social and political tension, and it also exacerbates the division between the formal and informal sectors—one of the key factors affecting the country's competitiveness.

Indeed, Turkey presents a very mixed picture in terms of the benefits it provides to workers and social services in general. As in America, the safety net works best for those in registered employment and fails many who are structurally unemployed. There is almost no extreme ("food") poverty, but the UNDP estimated in 2007 that 10 percent of the population earned less than $4.30 a day and that 19 percent of the population, measured by both food and nonfood consumption, lived in poverty—a situation aggravated by the breakdown of traditional support mechanisms. The government's attempts at poverty reduction have had mixed results. Since 1992 a "green card" system entitled the worst-off in society to free medical services and, according to figures for 2006, over ten million people, or 14 percent of the population, benefited. However, studies suggest some 21 percent of green-card holders earn above the poverty threshold, indicating the system provides both wide-scale abuse and an unacknowledged subsidy to the unregistered economy.

At the same time, a third of the 30 percent poorest in society had no health coverage at all. Similar anomalies attend a technically bankrupt social security system. Until recently, retirement was based on how many years you worked, rather than a pensionable age—which in practice meant men and women could stop working in their mid-forties, receive a modest stipend, and take on a second job.

Despite public opposition, the retirement age will rise, and by 2048 it is projected to reach sixty-five.[2]

Concern that the Europe with which Turkey does half its trade will be slow to recover its purchasing power has justified efforts to cultivate alternative partners in Latin America, the Middle East, and Africa, as well as to focus on trade with not-always-Western-friendly energy producers like Iran or Russia. This has similarities with Turkish attempts to target the emerging consumer markets in Central Asia in the 1990s, an initiative that, despite many successes, was ultimately constricted by a paucity of Turkish investment capital. Recent political turmoil in the MENA (Middle East–North Africa)—known as the "Arab Spring"—may have strengthened Turkish claims to regional leadership in the long run, but these events also suggest that finding reliable alternatives to EU markets is not so simple a matter. Turkey aggressively markets its goods and services, but levels of personal savings are low. The country itself is dependent on capital inflows to finance worryingly large current account deficits (the difference between what it exports and imports). This ultimately limits its influence abroad and means that it is reliant on its reputation for prudent financial management if it is to continue to attract investment for growth.

The European Union demands that Turkey introduce reforms to increase transparency, including the way public contracts are tendered and procured, along with regulation to end private-sector subsidies. Ultimately, however, if Turkey is to remain competitive it will have to retool to compete with the very countries it now claims to bridge.[3] Leading business conglomerates in Turkey now endow private universities, a trend that is symptomatic of the awareness that education, research, and development are one solution. Another is developing Istanbul as a regional financial center. The city is already served by well-regulated capital markets (daily trading volumes on the Istanbul Stock Exchange were on the order of $1.5 billion in 2010) as well as by a national airline that has aggressively expanded its network of destinations while other carriers have been in decline. Istanbul advertises itself as being within three hours of fifty-five countries. To cite the modest example of my own profession, not all that long ago the Western press would cover Turkish news from Athens or Rome. Now, as often as not, it is Istanbul-based correspondents who cover the debt crisis in Greece, the Russian invasion of Georgia, or developments in Baghdad and Islamabad.

If Turkey is an emerging market, what has it emerged from?

"We resemble ourselves," was Atatürk's rejoinder in the 1920s to those trying to lure Turkey into choosing between rival capitalist and socialist camps. Instead, the state was enshrined as a pragmatic agent, trying to resuscitate a war-damaged economy. Turkish suspicion of foreign presence in the economy dates from the final days of the empire when the Great Powers forced the bankrupt Ottomans to surrender major trading concessions. The central Ottoman Bank was largely British-owned, while the French operated the tobacco monopoly to recover their debts. One of the country's largest private banks began life on the orders of Atatürk, using as capital the gold collected by the Indian Muslim community to support the Turkish War of Independence. Nominally independent but state-owned firms manufactured steel; refined and sold petroleum; stitched, cobbled, and sold office attire; and distilled rakı (a.k.a. "the national tipple"—an anise-flavored spirit).

More to the point, private industry flourished under state protection. A number of today's major industrialists consolidated their fortunes during a period of high import tariffs, many of them producing foreign goods under license, in a system referred to as "import-substituting industrialization." While this may have been necessary to nurture fledgling industry, it was a strategy inevitably subsidized by the Turkish consumer paying over the odds for toothpaste, cars, or margarine. This inward-looking economy was ironically dependent on imports of secondary goods and scarcely survived the foreign exchange bottlenecks and the rise in petroleum prices of the 1970s. This was a turbulent period of Turkish history when rightist and leftist gangs fought for control of new urban neighborhoods established as a result of rural in-migration. The response was a military coup in 1980 that ushered in a period of authoritarian rule but also one of economic liberalization.

Under a program designed by technocrat-turned-politician Turgut Özal, the economy became more export-oriented and interest rates were allowed to float. Özal became premier when multiparty democracy was restored in 1983 and then president in 1989, and he continued to push Turkey into the global economy. By the mid-1980s the lira became fully convertible and by 1989 capital flowed freely in and out of the country. The small stamp duty Turks still pay when they travel abroad is a vestige of a bygone era when it was a crime for Turks to own foreign currency and there were limits to the amount they could take abroad. It was this closed economy that was symbolically laid to rest when Turkey entered into a customs union with the European Union in 1996 and when the lira was allowed to float freely in 2001.

If the international investment community compares Turkey to other sovereign markets, Turks themselves have not forgotten the high volatility of their own recent past. What elsewhere in the world was called the "roaring 1990s"—as the tech boom and housing boom both began to grow—is remembered in Turkey as the "lost decade" during which the country paid a premium for its inability to carry out root-and-branch reform.

At the time, the economy offered extravagant rewards for those able to ride out the cycles of boom and bust. Soon after the Istanbul Stock Exchange (ISE) started trading in 1986, it became notorious for being the best-performing emerging market one year and the worst-performing the next. Money flowed into Turkey, attracted by enormously high rates of interest on government debt. These high rates were financed by those on fixed incomes or with no savings—through chronic double- and sometime triple-digit inflation and declining purchasing power. Turkey is a Muslim-majority country and while the public takes for granted the reality of (un-Islamic) bank interest, it did not take a theologian to see that something was unjust in a system where the least well-off carried the greatest burden.

Economists pointed to what became known as the "inflation lobby." Supermarkets made more on investing the cash in their tills than they did by selling food. A blanket guarantee on deposits, intended to restore confidence after a sharp devaluation of the lira in 1994, created a gross moral hazard as bank licenses were distributed as political favors.

Banking consisted of little else than collecting deposits to lend to the government at very advantageous interest rates. At the same time, ordinary citizens became experts in arbitraging currencies, changing pensions and salaries into dollars or Deutsche Marks and then back into lira as the need arose. Small- and medium-sized Turkish businesses survived these vicissitudes by hard work, investing only from their own profits, and avoiding taxes. To this day, a large and unregistered "black" economy competes on unequal terms with those who pay their dues.

Even after the great warning bell of the 1994 economic crisis, Turkey was reluctant to reform. Too many people had become much too skilled at making the old engine work. However, that system came to a juddering halt with the collapse of the currency in 2001. Then, an IMF-supported disinflation program went badly wrong. It had been designed to reverse an unsustainable debt dynamic, but news of dissent within the government itself caused the markets to panic. For a brief period, interest rates soared into thousands of percentage points and some two dozen commercial banks bit the dust. The cost to the nation of meeting insured deposits and propping up state-owned banks was almost a third of GDP.

Turkey had no choice but to put its house in order. It did so with the help of what were referred to as the "twin external anchors." The first anchor was the IMF, which essentially took over the financing of Turkish debt from a wobbly financial sector. It committed Turkey to a program of reform, restored credibility, and reduced the cost of borrowing. The second was the European Union. At the 1999 Helsinki summit, Turkey was declared a candidate country and encouraged to go on a diet of political reform. That process continued unabated until 2005, when Turkey acquired a seat at the negotiating table. The Turkish lira shed six zeros, proof that the stabilization package and a program of genuine austerity had borne results. A new generation no longer thinks in terms of paying millions of lira for a loaf of bread. Turkey was fortunate in that it carried out its reform program at a time of high global liquidity. Direct foreign investment began to pour into the country as the dense cloud cover of chronic inflation that so obscured the Turkish market began to lift. A country which historically had trouble attracting even a billion dollars annually of direct foreign investment began to attract $20 billion in 2006 and even $15.7 billion in the crisis year 2008.

Turkey had understood the need to privatize its state-owned industries earlier than many of those countries that emerged from the former Soviet bloc, but successive governments only picked at reform, reluctant to surrender an important source of political patronage. Under IMF pressure, Turkey began to privatize the big ticket items, such as telecoms and petroleum refinery, although by this time the state sector's percentage share of the economy had already begun to shrink, overshadowed by the private sector.

In 2005, for the first time, Turkey finally completed an IMF standby package, which was extended for another three years. So by 2008 there was domestic pressure to turn to the IMF one more time as Turkey faced the crisis that resulted not from its own profligacy but from the collapse of the subprime market in New York. Markets held their breath while Turkey behaved like a developed economy and tried to spend its way out of a recession. The Central Bank eased monetary policy, the government eased fiscal policy, and the budget went deep into the red. Yet there was no loss of confidence and what had once been the "sick economy of Europe"—a play on the old designation of the late Ottoman Empire as the "sick man of Europe"—managed to steer its own way through the storm. And there was no need to bail out Turkish banks. Those which had survived the 2000–2001 domestic crisis were well-regulated and risk-adverse.

In short, Turkey has completed an important tier of reform, putting order to its banking system, awarding Central Bank independence (at least by comparison to a previous era), and asserting credible control over public finances. That it did so at gunpoint after a crisis in 2001 does not detract from that achievement.

However, Turkey now faces what economists refer to as a second generation of reform, involving the more intractable institutional problems. According to OECD reports, at the top of the list are the inflexibilities in the labor market, in which a protected formal sector encourages an unregistered economy. The tax burden, too, is regressive, with two-thirds collected from VAT or sales tax and one-third from direct taxation—the diametric opposite of the rest of the OECD countries.

Turkey's assertion that it has become an economic hub echoes its Cold War–era claim of having a geography crucial to the defense of the West. Politicians developed a sense of impunity not because Turkey was too *big* to fail, in the sense that it would drag down world financial institutions, but rather that it was too strategically important. Kemal Derviş, a former World Bank vice president who was parachuted into the Turkish treasury to rescue the economy in 2001, made no secret that his job of extracting a $16 billion rescue package from the IMF was made all the easier because the United States was eager to shore up its Turkish ally on the eve of its invasion of Iraq.

In the past Turkish politicians tried to bank on the country's geopolitical importance to avoid facing economic realities. Now, at last, it is the dog wagging the tail. Ankara has adopted a more assertive and independent foreign policy with the knowledge that an expanding and more confident economy will make its voice heard.

What is the GAP and why is it so controversial?

Water is the one resource advantage Turkey enjoys over its carbon-rich neighbors. Ankara has attempted to harness the headwaters of the Tigris and Euphrates rivers to provide hydroelectric power for the national grid as well as opportunity for the neglected, largely Kurdish, southeast region of the country. It does so through the Southeast Anatolian Project (or GAP, the Turkish acronym), which is like the Tennessee Valley Authority but infinitely more ambitious. The area it oversees is vast (30,000 square miles or 75,000 square kilometers, nearly as large as South Carolina or the Czech Republic), close to a tenth of the entire country both in area and population. While the full scope of the projected twenty-two dams and nineteen hydroelectric plants may never be realized, GAP has already changed the topography of the region, introducing vast lakes and even transforming the climate from arid to semitropical. It advertises itself as "a multi-sector, integrated and sustainable regional development project," restoring Turkey's slice of the Fertile Crescent to its former glory. Critics say it is putting the "mess" back into Mesopotamia.

Large development and dam projects worldwide are viewed with increasing skepticism from the viewpoint of cost/benefit, let alone concerns about the environment. This is amplified in the Turkish instance because of the politically sensitive area in which the GAP is situated. Some maintain that GAP threatens the water rights of downstream neighbors, Iraq and Syria; and they also suggest that, rather than developing the southeast of Turkey, it actually transfers resources (i.e., hydropower) to the developed western part of the country. There is concern that not enough has been done to prepare the population for the conversion to water-intensive farming or a transition away from cotton, which leaches the soil. One of the most persistent criticisms is that there is no water-pricing mechanism that would rationalize land use. Some Kurdish nationalists accuse the project of trying to divide and rule—literally—by crisscrossing the Kurdish homeland with water barriers, displacing people and flooding cultural landmarks.

There is no gainsaying that GAP's primary purpose is generating power for the rest of the country. Whereas 74 percent of the hydropower component of the project is complete, only 14 percent of the intended irrigation has been finished. However, it is also true that GAP is the principal development agency in an underdeveloped part of the country. Its proponents argue that it needs more teeth, not fewer, and that it had been eviscerated after its mandate expired in 2004, lingering on life support because it would be too politically sensitive to shut it down altogether. The project's social developments still provide window dressing for those who want to build more dams.

Irrigation had the immediate effect of raising per-capita income threefold when it was introduced in the 1990s to the Harran Plain, which may have been responsible for reducing political tension. Alongside hydroelectric projects are a score of social undertakings, including new universities, women's community centers, airfields that can be used to fly cut flowers to European markets, and even research into the habits of bees. The project's directors argue that its sophisticated water management provides a steady flow downstream and is actually in Syria's and Iraq's interests. Rates of evaporation in deep and cooler Turkish reservoirs are up to five times slower than facilities downstream beyond its border. This regulated flow, they maintain, more than compensates for reductions in the flow of water diverted for irrigation.

Even so, international sensitivities have meant that GAP hydroelectric projects have been hard to finance. Atatürk Dam—the 10.9-billion-kilowatt centerpiece of the project—was locally funded, and at the time of its completion in 1992 was estimated to have accounted for a third of Turkey's then 70 percent rate of inflation. The $1.5 billion Birecik Dam was built through a self-financing model (build-operate-transfer), which ultimately passed on its costs to the consumer through a high per-unit cost of electricity. The Ilısu Dam on the Tigris—a pure hydroelectric project—was originally proposed in 1954 but had its groundbreaking ceremony in 2006, soon after which work was suspended. The 3.8-billion-kilowatt dam will flood Hasankeyf, a rich archaeological site whose most visible stratum is a medieval Arab settlement. In 2002 campaigners were successful in getting British and Italian partner companies to withdraw from the $1.6 billion project and in 2009 German, Swiss, and Austrian export credit agencies finally withdrew their support after failing to receive adequate guarantees. Ankara declares itself determined to plow on with finance from domestic banks.

Part of this determination comes from government fondness for big projects. The State Hydraulic Works (DSI) is a powerful agency that historically has controlled about a third of the national investment budget. Süleyman Demirel, a former Turkish president, was once its head, and his predecessor, Turgut Özal, worked as an electrical engineer on the

Keban Dam on the Euphrates. The DSI directors have stated publicly their intention to dam every viable waterway in Turkey by 2030. This is clearly hubris but at least suggests that the Kurdish areas have not been picked out for special attention. The Çoruh River Development Plan in the Black Sea region, if completed in full, will consist of thirteen dams. Here, profitability is skewed by the need for an expensive road-building program that will inflate the per-unit cost of electricity. This has produced a civil protest movement whose argument is that sustainable tourism should be a greater priority than ultimately unsustainable hydropower. The World Water Tribunal has criticized the government's waiver of an environmental impact assessment as well as its sidestepping of the requirement to put projects out to competitive tender. The main criticism is that Turkey's dam building is done without real consultation with the affected populations. Some argue that Turkey deliberately avoids developing its huge potential for solar energy as this would render many of the small hydroprojects economically unviable.

How important is agriculture to the Turkish economy?

No respectable neighborhood in Turkey is without its weekly produce market where shoppers mark the passing of the seasons by changes in the rich array of domestically grown fruit and vegetables. Artichokes not cuckoos, mark the coming of spring, and persimmons and pomegranates the advent of autumn. Large swaths of Turkey are under cultivation: 27 million hectares or 105,000 square miles, equivalent to over 15 percent of the total agricultural land of the European Union. Turkey is the world's largest producer of hazelnuts and dried figs; other major exports include raisins and apricots. Cotton, sugar beet, wool, tomato for tomato paste, and tobacco are other leading commercial crops along with olives, pulses, cereals, citrus, and other perishable fruits and vegetables. There are said to be around 140 generic varieties of marketable fruits and vegetables worldwide; Turkey grows 80 of them.[4]

Yet for all that, the postwar history of Turkey has been one of agrarian decline. Though the sector actually grew in 2009 by 3.5 percent (in a year when the rest of the economy was affected by world recession), its overall weight in the economy has fallen to under 10 percent of GDP. However, for what will soon be a trillion dollar economy, that is still a big number. The agricultural lobby still exhibits considerable political muscle, given that the sector employs a quarter of the workforce overall and sustains rural constituencies. The introduction of tractors and mechanized farming produced the great sea change in the rural-to-urban ratio during the 1950s. Turkey continues to face the enormous challenge of protecting rural communities while not insulating farmers from market forces, and it does not appear yet to have got the balance right. The price of meat and dairy goods has fluctuated widely in recent years to the detriment of both producer and consumer. Part of the problem is that sheep-herding villages in Eastern Turkey have been forcibly depopulated as part of the strategy to fight the Kurdish insurgency and to deny rural guerrillas a base. Villagers were forbidden to take their animals to highland pastures. However, in general, Turkey maintains an expensive food policy in order to prevent even greater migration to the cities. Turkey may have a customs union on manufactured goods with Europe, but agriculture remains heavily protected. Many believe

Ankara would do well to reduce high-import tariffs and modify an out-of-date commitment to food self-sufficiency to one of food security. Rural inefficiency is paid for by the urban consumer.

Inefficiency is often explained by the dominance of small producers. Only 6 percent of farms are larger than 50 acres and 65 percent are smaller than 12.5 acres. This is in part a legacy of the lack of Latin American–style *latifundia* or a European landed aristocracy (Ottoman notables were more tax collectors than landowners) as well as of inheritance laws that until recently worked to subdivide holdings. Another culprit is vacillating public policy. The state-owned Agricultural (Ziraat) Bank until 2001 had a statutory obligation to make risky loans to farmers. At one point Turkey adopted the EU policy of subsidizing farmers' incomes, a fairer system than paying support for individual crops, but then it reverted back to the old system.

The dramatic increase in world commodity prices, including foodstuffs, would suggest Turkey can and should arrest its agrarian decline. Farming is becoming ever more sophisticated; for example, plastic tunneling is now a common sight as farmers try to take advantage of higher prices for nonseasonal produce. However, European- or American-style agroindustrial estates are still not common, even in land irrigated by the GAP administration. The principle beneficiary of irrigation schemes has been the Harran Plain, located along the Syrian border. While average land holdings there are larger than in Turkey generally, sharecropping is widespread and there is no real land consolidation or reform. One of the benefits of the initial rapprochement between Ankara and Damascus (see below) is that it would lead to the demining of the 510-mile-long (822 kilometer)

Syrian border and open a huge tract of long-fallow land to high-value organic farming. In general, the success of large-scale investments that would revive Turkish agriculture await a new generation of farm managers.

What are the differences between Istanbul and Ankara?

It is impossible to imagine a harem girl keeping a tryst in the back alleys of Ankara, because there are no back alleys. Most of Turkey's capital was built after a city ordinance that, in the interest of creating European-style boulevards, actually forbade the construction of culs-de-sac. Ankara is more than happy to cultivate this reputation for being one long, unambiguous corridor of power. It owes its status as a capital to the fact that it was far enough inland to be defendable and yet still accessible by rail at the time the Republic was declared. While the citadel dates back at least to the late Bronze Age, the rest of the city is one of the twentieth century's first purpose-built capitals (Canberra is earlier), a deliberate attempt to realign the geography of political power away from the Levantine and cosmopolitan cities of the coast and into the Anatolian heartland. With their flat and occasionally leaky roofs, the new government buildings owed more to the Bauhaus than Sinan, the architect synonymous with the classical Ottoman age. Ankara, in effect, became a citadel of Turkish nationalism.

In time, Istanbul became grateful that the politicians left. The city's loss of political power did nothing to damage its status as Turkey's cultural and commercial capital. Once, Istanbul might have seemed a world both geographically and culturally aloof from the rest of the country, but it is now a city of over 13 million. This means that approximately one in every six Turkish citizens lives in what has become a microcosm of the country as a whole. Istanbul accounts for well over a quarter of GDP, pays 40 percent of the nation's taxes, and accounts for 60 percent of the trade.

The rejiggering of the political map at the end of the Cold War established Istanbul as the regional hub of a newly defined Eurasian economic zone. This, the city elders hope, will provide a springboard for it to realize its ultimate ambition of becoming a world financial center in the style of London or Hong Kong. While OECD annual reports praise the emergence of alternative "growth nodes" in Turkey and a new breed of provincial enterprises run by "Anatolian Tigers," this has not weakened Istanbul's pull. New money competes with old to buy into the Istanbul boom.

Without Ankara as an alternative growth pole, Istanbul would have been larger still. "Istanbul good, Ankara bad" became the watchword of Istanbul's business community, and this was more than the usual private-sector gripe that government was dousing its entrepreneurial flair. It described, in part, the real cost to the economy of successive governments that merely tinkered with reform. It also described a highly centralized notion of power that radiates from the top down and is legitimated by its ideological purity rather than by popular mandate. Ankara is suspicious of the process of globalization that eats away at its own power, failing to understand that the European Union is a body more bureaucratic than it could ever hope to be. By comparison, Ankara means filling a form in triplicate.

Grace Ellison, an intrepid English reporter who made her way to Ankara on the eve of Turkish independence in 1923, described the city as a "private club to which one gains admittance by being in sympathy with Turkey's bid for freedom. ... If you were not trusted you would not be allowed over the threshold." Ankara still preserves that club-like atmosphere, even if it has had to accommodate a far greater variety of members. Those early ministry buildings have been replaced with towering office blocks, but the city is still a political hothouse, taking far more seriously than Istanbul challenges to the core identity of the Turkish state and social movements and economic currents outside its control. The suspicion of non-insiders extends not just to decadent Istanbul but at times even to its own government. This sense of cliquishness is not improved by judges living in housing cooperatives with other judges and military officers with officers, though MPs no longer have their own dedicated housing estate.

Istanbul, too, has changed. What were once low-density neighborhoods of in-migrants are being redeveloped into commercial and residential-tower blocks, many of them constructed by the government public housing agency (TOKİ). The city's upper-crust citizens are drifting into their own gated communities away from established neighborhoods where all social classes lived side by side.

From the beginning, both Istanbul and Ankara were subject to the phenomenon that was to determine the characteristics of major Turkish cities—the unplanned, often illegal neighborhoods of squatters in the city periphery. This accelerated during the 1950s. Ankara, the model capital, became in effect an unwitting model of a process that would undermine its own authority. The new state could change the alphabet, but it had a much harder time implementing a city plan. Well over half of the residential units in all major Turkish cities have been built in some sort of defiance of planning permission. Some luxury housing does not have occupancy permits, and banks are even prepared to finance construction not in conformity with the rules. This suggests that a highly centralized Turkish state has been built on rules made to be broken.

There is a culture of complicity in which citizens turn a blind eye to others' wrongdoing because they hope to get away with their own. A mountain of regulations exists to protect the environment and natural and historical values, but a bird's-eye view of any Turkish city suggests those rules are there to line the pockets of those charged with enforcing them. The great example was in the 1994 local election, when current Prime Minister Recep Tayyip Erdoğan was running for mayor of İstanbul. Newspapers reported with shock and horror that he had built houses without planning permission. According to most psephologists, this almost certainly increased his vote. Indeed, when asked in debate with other candidates whether he would destroy illegal (*gecekondu*) housing, he replied, "No, I live in one." Another Istanbul mayor, Ahmet Isvan, elected in 1973, was photographed with a sledgehammer destroying a mafia-built casino, striking fear into the hearts of ordinary people whose houses were also illegally built. He was not renominated as the Republican People's Party (CHP) candidate in 1977.

Of course both the passing years and technology have literally and figuratively shortened the distance between the two cities (as a journalist, I recall an Istanbul bank president boasting to me that he had never set foot in Ankara's beehive of impropriety and cronyism, then interrupted our interview first to take a call from a government minister and then from the governor of the Central Bank). Many businesses maintain an office in Ankara to keep an eye on what's happening in parliament and in the courts. Certain political parties are by nature more "Istanbul" than "Ankara." There is little doubt to which city the Republican People's Party (CHP), the party of the Revolution, owes its primary allegiance, but for most of the last decade Turkey has been run by a party whose leader started out as mayor of Istanbul. If party politics has been successful in quelling the old bureaucracy this is in part because it has harnessed the economic power of Istanbul to retake the citadel of power.

4
TURKEY IN THE WORLD

Where does Turkey fit into the world?

A map is the obvious place to see where Turkey fits in the
world. It lies at the intersection of several overlapping
regions—the Balkans, the Caucasus, the Middle and Near
East, and the Eastern Mediterranean. However, the maps
made by satellite imaging are not necessarily the maps that
people have in their minds. Cartoonist Saul Steinberg's
famous *New Yorker* magazine cover, *View of the World from
9th Avenue,* parodied the provincialism that lurks beneath
Manhattan's conviction of its own sophistication. How
would a Turkish Steinberg depict the view from Turkey?

The answer is surprisingly complicated. There are 5 million
ethnic Turks living in Europe, and Turkey is a candidate for
the European Union. Therefore, what happens in Brussels
and the rest of the continent matters. Turkey has borders
with Iran and Syria, and tries to find a modus vivendi with
countries the United States regards with suspicion. Turkey
was one of the first states to recognize the State of Israel but
is a stronger supporter of Palestine. Turkish peacekeeping
troops have participated in UN- and NATO-led missions in
the Balkans, Afghanistan, and even Somalia. While ties with

Greece are on the mend, there are still disputes over airspace and continental shelf boundaries in the Aegean. There have been Turkish troops stationed in Northern Cyprus since 1974, and recently discovered natural gas in the Eastern Mediterranean has become the cause for renewed tension with the Greek Republic in the south.

No country on earth can ignore what happens in Washington, and after the 2003 U.S. invasion of Iraq, Turkey suddenly found America in its own backyard. Turkey has tried to cultivate a special relationship with its ethnic cousins in the energy-rich new nations of Central Asia. Turkish contractors operate in Libya, and Turkish textile manufacturers invest in Egypt to take advantage of that country's free trade agreement with the United States. Conflict between Armenia and Azerbaijan complicate Ankara's options on its northeastern frontier. It also shares a border with Georgia, so when Russian troops marched into South Ossetia in 2008 Turks snapped to attention. Russia is Turkey's largest individual trading partner, part of the equation of Turkish efforts to be a key transit hub for gas and oil, but Russia works to exclude Turkish influence from its "near abroad" and relations are not always easy. The Gulf States are importers of Turkish services and potential investors. Turkish diplomats and traders have gone on a charm offensive, opening missions and embassies in Latin American and African countries that were once well beyond the Turkish purview. And so the list goes on. A Turkish Steinberg might, therefore, put Turkey at the center of a complex universe. "If the world had a capital, it would be Istanbul," is a much-quoted but almost certainly apocryphal maxim attributed to Napoleon.

Western editorialists, by contrast, are often tempted to see Turkey in a much simpler context. The question that concerns them most is whether the Islamic beliefs of Turkey's population mean the country is destined to slip away from the Western bloc. They speak of "losing Turkey" or of Turkey shifting its axis eastward. Many, of course, understand that the choices facing Turkey are not Manichaean, a clash of civilizations between East and West, but rather are based on a nuanced calculation of where the country's best interests lie. Even so, many observers wonder if Turkey is not making the wrong choices—its judgment clouded by a determination to reassert a regional role in the old Ottoman domains where it exercises a cultural affinity, but at the expense of its Western allies. The Turkish response to such criticism is that its traditional allies have so mismanaged their relations in the Middle and Near East that they should be grateful to Turkey for assuming some of the burden.

I once put the Steinberg question to Gürbüz Doğan Ekşioğlu, an artist from a small Black Sea town that is about as far from the Algonquin Round Table as you can get. Even so, it was his drawing of the Manhattan skyline, with all of its innumerable buildings twinned, that appeared on the *New Yorker's* cover for the second anniversary of 9/11. His view of his own society was that of the Steinberg cartoon stood on its head—that many Turks had a clearer and more sympathetic view of what was happening across continents than what was happening in a neighborhood a few blocks away.

How did Turkey respond to the end of the Cold War?

Up until 1989, the Turkish view of the world was a great deal simpler. The country was from NATO's perspective the archetypal Cold War warrior, the lonely sentinel on the southern flank. Ankara kept a distance from the conflicts in the Middle

East, relieved that the Iran-Iraq war of 1980–1988 resulted in neither side getting the upper hand. However, after the collapse of the Soviet Empire, the entire political geography of its region changed. Turkey, a nation once on the periphery of the Western alliance, suddenly discovered the former Soviet states of Uzbekistan, Kazakhstan, Turkmenistan, and Azerbaijan. It felt cultural and ethnic affinities with these countries but also was only just learning to find them on a map. Nonetheless, while Turkey sought economic opportunities with its new neighbors, this was very far from the peace dividend to which it felt entitled for helping to win the Cold War. Indeed, Turkey had the sense of being overtaken by the very Warsaw Pact against which it had once stood guard. In 1993, even as the Czech Republic and Slovakia agreed to go their separate ways in the Velvet Revolution, Turkey's battle with Kurdish separatists in the southeast of the country was spiraling out of control. In 1997 the European Union began accession negotiations not just with the Visegrád Group of countries of Central Europe but also with Cyprus—a country in which Turkish troops were enforcing the division of the island in the interest of protecting Turkish Cypriots. This was the same year that the Turkish military was busy undermining its own democratically elected but Islamic-led coalition. In this uncertain climate, at times Ankara appeared to cling to the waning certainties of the Cold War with the tenacity of a soldier refusing to lay down his arms.

Turkey's sense of isolation also derived from the fact that its principal coinage—its strategic importance to its Western allies—had been devalued by the removal of the Soviet threat. Turkey had asserted that importance somewhat at its own expense. Indeed, part of its leverage in international affairs was that its allies treated it with kid gloves, uncertain that Ankara would reliably behave in its own best interests. At times it even appeared as if Turkey, in the throes of the social upheavals resulting from its own modernization, was braced and sustained by the tension of the Cold War. Economists speak of hydrocarbon-rich nations as having the "petrol curse," which skews their development. Turkey had the strategic curse, an assumption of self-importance that appeared to restrict its institutional growth, rationalize a reluctance to reform, and limit its administrative capacity.

The West may have needed Turkey as a forward base against the Soviet Union—and may rely on it still as an ally against Iran—but more to the point, it wanted a trouble-free Turkey on its side. No sooner had the Soviet Union collapsed than Saddam Hussein marched into Kuwait. Turkey was thus presented with an opportunity to reinvent itself as a strategic asset by providing logistic support to the U.S.-led coalition, against the advice of its own military. President Turgut Özal initiated what was called "an active foreign policy." At the time, his intention (many believed) was to control access to the oil fields in Kirkuk in the north of Iraq—a region to which Turkey has a historic claim. In practice, the American invasion proved inconclusive. Turkey was obliged to impose an embargo against what had been the extremely lucrative Iraqi market and (in order to staunch the flow of refugees) guarantee de facto autonomy for Iraq's Kurds.

Washington took for granted that Turkey would cooperate in the second invasion of Iraq in 2003, and the newly elected government gave every signal that it would give permission for American troops to transit through Turkish territory. However, as much through happenstance as design, the new government mismanaged a parliamentary vote and was obliged to refuse. While this was not the end of Turkey's strategic relationship with the United States, nor even the first major disagreement between the two allies, renunciation of its strategic importance undoubtedly set new parameters. And while it might sound strange to claim that the Cold War ended in Turkey a decade later than the rest of Europe, the war in Iraq, coinciding as it did with other major events, had a transformative effect on a par with the dismantling of the Berlin Wall.

That war was itself, of course, the by-product of the United States' change in perception of its own strategic priorities after the 9/11 attacks. The year 2001 is remembered in Turkey with little affection for an entirely different reason. On February 21, or Black Wednesday, as it is now known in Turkey, an argument between the president and his cabinet over corruption spilled into the press and sparked a contagion in the markets. The Turkish economy went into free fall; interest rates soared and the lira halved in value. Confidence in public administration was already at a historic low, following an earthquake in August 1999 in the developed western part of the country. This had resulted in huge destruction and the loss of more than 18,000 lives around the epicenter in Izmit. The 1999 quake exposed not just the government's inability to cope but also an entire postwar system of skewed urban development and municipal graft.

Not surprisingly, Turks were anxious for a new broom to sweep politics clean. No political party which had won seats in the 1998 general election managed to win any seats at all in the following election in 2002. The overwhelming beneficiary was the Justice and Development Party—better known by its Turkish acronym AK—a newly formed group that understood not just the domestic mood for reform but also international expectations involving Turkey's place in the world. The AK Party secured reelection in 2007 and again in 2011, each time with an increased share in the popular vote.

What changes has the AK Party made?

The AK Party is the latest in a succession of parties descended from an overtly Islamic movement founded in the 1960s. However, the party set itself a reformist agenda in an attempt to capture the political middle ground. The party's charismatic leader, Tayyip Erdoğan, began his career in the youth movement of a nationalist Islamic party. A youthful Erdoğan had once been photographed sitting at the feet of the proto-Taliban Afghan warlord Gulbeddin Hekmatyar. (But then, Ronald Reagan had started political life as a Democrat.) Erdoğan had undergone almost as profound a transformation to become the able mayor of Istanbul, a megacity larger than many European countries. The AK Party describes itself as being socially conservative but it rejects the notion that it is Islamic or Islamist or even "Islamic democrat" (in the way that German and northern European parties, for example, are Christian Democrats), mindful of Turkish law that forbids the exploitation of religion for political ends.

Instead, the AK Party defined being more open about religion in public life as part of a more general struggle to make Turkey more fully democratic. At the same time, it gives the wink to the conservative and religious inclinations of their supporters. The body language says, "Trust us, we're on your side." This continues to prompt suspicion that the party has a hidden Islamic agenda or that the bulk of its supporters regard their own particular rights as more important than democratic rights in general. Even so, the rhetoric meant the AK Party was less prone to beat the drum of Turkish nationalism and intrinsically more tolerant of those seeking other freedoms—including the right to think of oneself as Kurdish.

In 2002, when first elected, the AK Party was trying to pull the economy out of economic crisis, and it was necessary to maintain market credibility and rally international support. The argument the AK Party was able to make to its Western allies was that it alone could keep Turkey's commitments to the IMF or push for EU entry precisely because the party had the zeal of the (in this case) unconverted. It alone, according to its leaders, understood the conservative impulses of the country and could lead the country back to the moderate high ground. Turkey, under AK party rule, began to acquire a symbolic importance to the West, no longer viewed as a physical bulwark to an external threat but rather as a soft power able to set a good example. Turkey would demonstrate that it was possible to locate democratic traditions within an Islamic-influenced political culture. And it could demonstrate to its eastern neighbors that there was no inimical Western hostility to Islam.

For the AK Party, this became a prima facie case of being careful about what it wished for. Certainly one of the party's priorities after coming to power was to shake off its reputation as Washington's Islamist poodle. The AK Party's opponent, a traditional establishment that includes the military, was also a segment of society that regarded itself as the gatekeeper of modernity and Western values. They felt this role being usurped and looked for a motive behind the West's betrayal of them in favor of the AK Party. The reasons, they thought, became crystal clear when European politicians spoke in defense of Kurdish rights or U.S. Congressmen lobbied for recognizing genocide in the fate of the Armenian population in 1915. The West, Turkey's nationalist opposition argued, was trying to achieve by stealth the work it started with World War I—that of fatally undermining the integrity of the nation. This explains the seemingly counterintuitive finding of Turkish public opinion surveys: the further up the social scale, the more support for rejecting the European Union.[1]

The AK Party came to power because the postwar Turkish political machine had collapsed. After two terms in power its leaders had managed to reconstruct it. They did so partly by turning the growth of Turkish cities and the demand for houses and urban services into votes. In the first eight years of AK rule, TOKİ, the state housing authority, built just under half a million homes, literally constructing its own constituency.

As the AK Party became more entrenched, it became more confident and more assertive in its dealings with the world. In 2009, the éminence grise of Turkish foreign policy, professor of international relations Ahmet Davutoğlu, was made foreign minister. He was accompanied into office by two sound bites of his own creation. The first came from the title of his book, *Strategic Depth*, which suggested that Turkey would no longer be the handmaiden of someone else's world vision but master of its own. Moreover, it should exercise soft power not on behalf of the West but on its own behalf in a broad section of the globe where, either because of an Ottoman past or a common Islamic heritage, it had a cultural affinity. The second catchphrase was a policy called "zero problems with neighbors." This was a reworking of the Atatürkist mission statement of Turkish foreign policy, which was "peace at home, peace in the world." The old Turkey was an island of stability in a sea of troubles, which preserved its integrity despite its unfriendly neighborhood. The new Turkey was about constructing bridges.

Professor Davutoğlu set about building up Turkey's reputation and enlarging his own carbon footprint with an endless diplomatic globe trot from Brasilia to Beirut, Washington to Beijing. However, Turkey's own high opinion of its role was not necessarily shared by its postwar allies. We have WikiLeaks to thank for a former American ambassador's faint praise of Ankara's desire to play a regional role with "Rolls Royce ambitions but Rover resources." Turkey initially appeared far more successful in reducing tensions with neighbors like Iran and Syria than with countries like Armenia where particularly the United States had a more pressing interest it succeed. After years of hostility with Syria—even issuing a démarche threatening invasion in 1998 over Damascus's support for Kurdish rebels—Turkey brought about a dramatic rapprochement. Southeastern cities like Gaziantep and şanlıurfa welcomed hordes of Syrian shoppers, in search of goods they couldn't buy at home, who were bussed across the border without having to obtain visas. At the same time, talks with the European Union went into neutral, attempts to reopen the border with Armenia stalled, and relations with Israel went into sharp decline (see below). "Zero problems with neighbors" increasingly became redefined as "zero problems with some neighbors." Revolution in the Arab world complicated matters further as Ankara openly questioned the legitimacy of the Bashar al-Assad regime in Syria. The unilateral declaration of sanctions and stationing troops on the border was more than an exercise of soft power and put Turkey in direct confrontation with Iran, a committed backer of al-Assad. And yet, as the Middle East–North Africa countries appeared to be in the throes of a transformation as profound as the collapse of the Soviet bloc, the Turkish model again became attractive as an example of a country where changed occurred incrementally and at the ballot box.

How strong is the U.S.-Turkish alliance?

Were there such a thing as a division of labor between Brussels and Washington over how to deal with Turkey, Washington would have the easier job. Europe is negotiating Turkish membership of the European Union, a process that means sharing sovereignty and harmonizing institutions. There is no question of Turkey becoming the fifty-first state of the United States. If Washington sometimes seems more enthusiastic about Turkish membership of the European Union than Europe itself, it is because it sees membership as bestowing that most valuable of characteristics: stability. It views Ankara primarily as a piece in the strategic puzzle of NATO's common defense. Historically and logically, the U.S.-Turkish relationship is strongest when common security concerns are greatest; it becomes attenuated when the threat level goes down. And there is a great deal of posturing in between.

Turkey may be one of the few countries where the United States enjoys a healthy trade surplus. Even so, the U.S. market accounted for only 3.3 percent of total Turkish exports in 2008 and 5.9 percent of imports with a trade volume of $14.3 billion. And even here defense-related expenditure and procurement play an important role—Turkey, for example, builds F1-16 fighter aircraft under license from Lockheed Martin. Many American companies deal with Turkey through European, particularly Dutch, subsidiaries so the real figures are higher than the official ones suggest.

Modern Turkish-U.S. relations have their symbolic beginning on April 5, 1946, when the *USS Missouri* moored off the Bosphorus to return the remains of Münir Ertegün, the Turkish ambassador (and father of Atlantic Records' founder Ahmet Ertegün). The mission was intended to cement Turkey's adherence to the postwar Western alliance. Ankara was anxious to be wooed. Turkey had been neutral until 1945, escaping not impoverishment but certainly the destruction it had suffered in and after World War I. A time-honored stratagem of playing the great powers against one another no longer worked in a world divided into two camps. The Soviet Union posed an immediate threat to Turkey by refusing to renew the Turkish-Soviet friendship pact until there was a renegotiation of the common border established in 1921. More ominously, Stalin pressed for participation in the defense of the Bosphorus and Dardanelles Straits. The Truman Doctrine was subsequently formulated, in 1947, to keep Turkey as well as Greece within the Western sphere, and Turkey became a recipient of Marshall Aid the following year.

Turkey's participation in the Korean War (the Turkish Brigade famously lost 400 lives defending the American Eighth Army's retreat after the 1950 defeat at the Battle of the Ch'ongch'on River)—indeed, one could argue, even its move toward multiparty democracy—was intended to secure for itself a place under the NATO umbrella. Today, Turkey reluctantly accepts that it should participate in a NATO missile shield that would protect Europe from Iranian attack. In 1963 Ankara felt betrayed when President Kennedy withdrew Jupiter nuclear missiles from Turkey as a quid pro quo for the Soviet withdrawal of missiles from Cuba the previous year. The most famous example suggesting that Turkish and

U.S. interests would not always coincide came in 1964, when President Johnson warned Prime Minister İsmet İnönü not to intervene on behalf of Turkish Cypriots. The Johnson letter, still inscribed in Turkish memory, suggested that NATO would not be obliged to come to Turkey's rescue were the Soviet Union to use this as a pretext to invade.

Even a modicum of hindsight reveals that if Turkey is sometimes estranged from the West, it is part of an attempt to balance its own geostrategic interests within a complex alliance. When Turkey did intervene in Cyprus in 1974, the U.S. Congress, against the wishes of President Ford and Henry Kissinger, imposed an arms embargo. In 1980, Turkey's martial law president, General Evren, refused to cooperate with President Carter's bid to rescue American hostages in Tehran in order to prevent Turkey from becoming involved in the conflict. Again it was the Turkish military, far more critical than American neo-cons of the Islamic inclinations of its own politicians, who were chary of supporting the United States in Iraq both in 1991 and 2003. Their hesitation had little to do with solidarity for a fellow Muslim-majority nation, and everything to do with a fear that invasion would lead (as, indeed, it did) to an autonomous Iraqi Kurdish entity right on Turkey's border.

It is not surprising that Turks often display the ambivalence of many Europeans (or even many Americans) who prefer Americana to American policy—they admire the wide-finned Chevrolet but find the driving scary. Turkey accepts American soft power—using Intel chips to access Twitter, for example, or cheering the Detroit Pistons when Mehmet Okur was on the team and then transferring their allegiance when Okur moved over to the Utah Jazz. Turkish elites, no matter their political persuasion, shop in New York or Miami and send their children to Columbia or Tufts University. This is not to say they trust Washington's ability to run the world.

What is surprising, however, is the degree to which Turkish familiarity with America has bred contempt. Pew Global Attitude surveys show a growing disillusionment with the United States, far greater than the rest of Europe. Only 17 percent of those surveyed in 2010 had a positive opinion. One Ankara-based polling organization (MetroPOLL) released a study in early 2011 which said that 43 percent of Turks perceived the United States as the country's biggest threat. Only 3 percent of the survey saw Iran, despite its nuclear program, as being any threat at all. At some level, perhaps, there is a "real" America with which Turkey has both quarrels and mutual interests and a "fictive hegemonic" America which has come to represent Turkish frustrations with its own society. The contradiction is hinted at in one survey based on in-depth interviews, which in 2007 revealed that 80 percent of those interviewed saw the United States as a very substantial or major threat yet at the same time a quite large number (42 percent) thought Turkey was wrong in 2003 not to provide logistic support for U.S. troops in Iraq (compared to 49 percent who supported the decision). Even odder, 57 percent of those interviewed saw Christian missionaries as posing a threat to Turkey even though the number only slightly exceeds the perceived number of extraterrestrials.[2]

If America pops up as the villain in Turkish urban legend, it is because of the perception of the United States' interest in Turkey. For years it was a truism in Washington that the relationship between the Defense Department and the Turkish chiefs of staff took precedence over that between the State Department and the Turkish Ministry of Foreign Affairs. During Turkey's period of unstable coalition governments, there were concrete reasons for this, namely that the armed forces presented a coherent partner while the politicians did not. During the 1990s, for example, there were twelve different Turkish foreign ministers.

More to the point, Turks often assume that the United States empowers the Turkish military's sense of its own independence from democratic process. Few believe that their military would have unseated their own government in 1971 and again in 1980 without at the very least a silent nod from Washington. While annual State Department human rights reports drew attention to a culture of impunity that had taken root in the occurity forces in the aftermath of martial law, many Turks saw this as mere posturing. If some Turks blame their own sense of powerlessness on a "deep state" that frustrates the popular will, they feel certain that this inner cabal has a hotline to an office somewhere in the Pentagon.

Whatever the truth of such suspicions, we do have a very different picture, courtesy of the WikiLeaks disclosures, of a conversation between a U.S. diplomat and the Turkish deputy chief of staff at a tense moment in recent history. In 2007 the military issued a public warning to the government—delivered as a posting on the Armed Forces Internet site—not to betray the secular founding principles of the Constitution by electing an unsuitable president. In Turkish parlance, this was as good as threatening to send in the tanks if the government didn't behave. In an interview on May 23, 2007, the U.S. envoy Nancy McEldowney requested and received an assurance from the general seated across the table that the military would maintain their commitment to democracy and respect the result of an upcoming election.

The Unites States, knowingly or unwittingly, has been implicated in Turkey's domestic politics. The AK Party, soon after its launching in 2002, sought U.S. approval, and soon-to-be prime minister Erdoğan found doors in Washington open to him ahead of the election that year. His visit was packaged as a testimonial that the party had abandoned the anti-Western rhetoric in which many of its founders had been reared. However, Turkey's secular establishment saw this acceptance as proof that the AK Party was itself a creation of the United States. Indeed, one of the charges brought against the AK Party in 2008, when the public prosecutor called for it to be shut down, was that it had become the tool of American foreign policy.

The Iraq War in 2003 was seen as ignoring Turkey's interests and brutalizing the people of Iraq, and was the overriding reason for a sharp decline in the United States' popularity. A particular incident brought this home. On July 4, 2003, U.S. troops staged a spectacular raid on a band of Turkish special forces in Northern Iraq, bundling them into custody with bags over their heads as if they were exports to Guantanamo Bay. What the commandos were up to has still to be confirmed—it was reported that they were an assassination squad targeting a local Kurdish governor. And although the men were soon released, the episode went on to inspire a spate of *Rambo*-style revenge films and a bestselling novel in which a Turkish patriot avenges the American invasion of his country by detonating a nuclear device outside the White House. In 2004, members of the AK party government were equating the American-British assault on Fallujah with "genocide," and even the prime minister appeared to side with the insurgents when he referred to those killed as "martyrs."[3] In 2005 then Secretary of Defense Donald Rumsfeld was still blaming the tenacity of the Iraqi insurgency on that refusal by the Turkish parliament two years earlier to allow an infantry division to pass through Turkish soil at the time of the initial invasion.

At the end of the day, however, Washington does not allow itself the luxury of bearing a grudge. It set itself the improbable task of trying to construct a nation out of the ruins of Iraq and it would have been foolish to demonize Turkey, a country that resembled the stable democracy it hoped to build elsewhere. The conventional wisdom is that Turkey and the United States need one another in a treacherous corner of the globe. Barack Obama chose to visit Turkey on his first bilateral trip overseas as president, clearly hoping to mend fences damaged during the Bush presidency. Obama referred to U.S.-Turkey relations not in the Cold War language as a "strategic" partnership but as a "model partnership"—"in which a majority-Christian and a majority-Muslim nation—a Western nation and a nation that straddles two continents—can create a modern international community that is respectful, secure, and prosperous."[4] If Turkey had been the West's air force carrier during the Cold War, it was now more of a safe platform from which to view the safari park of wild nations.

The Obama administration's infatuation with Turkey turned slightly sour when Ankara broke ranks with its Western allies in 2010, voting as a nonpermanent member of the UN Security Council against imposing sanctions on Iran. Turkey's reasoning was that an economic embargo was unlikely to disarm Tehran's nuclear program and that it was indeed in the West's interest for Turkey to play the role of the good cop. Ankara's reluctance to define Iran as a security risk found little favor in Washington. From Washington's perspective, the "zero problems with neighbors" policy appeared to be a "de-securitization"[5] (in lay terms, "turning a blind eye") of some of the very issues in which Turkey was meant to pull its weight. As that policy became more difficult to enforce, as relations with Syria again began to deteriorate, and as Iran began to jockey more openly with Turkey for influence in the political order succeeding the Arab Spring, Ankara and Washington again drew closer together. In September 2011 Turkey announced it would be downgrading diplomatic relations with Israel as a reaction to the *Mavi Marmara* incident (see below). Yet, it declared almost in the same breath that it would agree to host radar installations to provide a shield for Europe (and in all probability, Israel) against a possible Iranian missile first strike. While at first glance this might seem to be throwing American public opinion a meaty bone to distract from its policy toward Israel, it was also a case of distracting its own public opinion so it could resecuritize (i.e., no longer ignore) the threat from Iran.

What is Turkey's relationship with Israel and what are its effects?

Turkey was among the first states to recognize Israel in 1949. The relationship was built on Turkish concerns that Nassarism and Arab nationalism would allow the Soviet Union to gain a toehold in the Eastern Mediterranean. Once upon a time (or at least in the 1950s), it was the United States that restrained Turkey from intervening militarily in Iraq. In 1957 Ankara mounted troops on the Syrian border to destabilize a coalition of Nassarites and pro-Communists. "If there is any reaction, it must be initiated by Arabs and not Turkey or Western powers," Secretary of State John Dulles cabled home during a visit to Ankara in 1958.[7]

The Palestinian question, posed in the wake of the 1967 Six-Day War, marked a shift in Turkish sympathies. Successive governments have had the task of balancing increasing domestic empathy with the Palestinian cause with the rewards of maintaining good relations with an influential Western-allied nation. The Turkish military, which has benefited from Israel's high-tech defense industry, is a key component of this equation. Yet, even it has wavered. Relations between Israel and Turkey were at a low point in the post-1980 period, when Turkey's martial law authority protested Israel's transfer of its capital from Tel Aviv to Jerusalem by reducing diplomatic representation to a second secretary. This was at a time when Turkey's own military government was isolated internationally and set out to attract Middle Eastern investment. Full normalization of relations only occurred in 1991. The following year Turkey publicly marked the 500th anniversary of the flight of Spanish Jews to the Ottoman Empire with a program of commemorative events. This was in part an attempt to woo Jewish and pro-Israeli lobbies in Washington to counter entrenched ethnic American Greek and Armenian opposition.

Conventional wisdom, certainly in Turkey, is that Israel needs Ankara more than the other way around. Turkey has in the past provided elbowroom—a nearby destination for Israeli tourists and open skies for Israeli fighter jets to train. At the same time, an Ankara able to speak to Israel presents a very different picture to the world than a Turkey that might adopt the anti-Zionist discourse of the Middle East. Ankara sees the Arab-Israeli conflict as dividing its own loyalties and has frequently, if optimistically, volunteered to play the role of honest broker. Unlike the United States, it sees itself as free of domestic constraints to criticize matters such as Israeli settlement policy, arguing that it does so in the interests of a greater peace.

As an institution, the AK Party is not intrinsically biased against Israel, although it does have the instincts to protect its base from encroachment by parties further to the religious right. The uproar that arose when AK party officials met with a Hamas delegation in 2005 was no greater than the decision in 1979 by the Republican People's Party (CHP) to allow Yasser Arafat to open a PLO office in Ankara. Bülent Ecevit, then prime minister, was again in office in 2002 when he accused the Sharon administration of pursuing policies tantamount to genocide. Even Necmettin Erbakan, whose Welfare Party had campaigned on cutting ties with Israel and fulminated against Zionists and sometimes even Jews, oversaw as prime minister in 1996 the implementation of both a free trade agreement with Israel and the joint production of air-to-ground missiles. Erbakan himself signed a contract with Israel Aircraft Industries to upgrade Turkish F-4 Phantom jets.[7] In 2007, the Erdoğan government invited Israeli president Shimon Peres to address the Turkish Grand National Assembly.

This provides some context for the recent poisoning of relations that began in 2008 in the wake of the Israeli military operation in the Gaza Strip, deplored in Turkey for the high number of civilian casualties. Prime Minister Erdoğan claimed a personal sense of betrayal. Trying to reconcile Israel to its neighbors was far from incidental to its "zero problems" policy. Bringing about a settlement between Israel and Syria was the glittering prize. This was the key irritant that kept the region inflamed. Turkish diplomats had been mediating between Syria and Israel before the Israeli action (although many believe those negotiations had already stalled).[8] In what became a notorious incident, Erdoğan claimed extra time at a meeting in February 2009 of the World Economic Forum in Davos, during which he harangued Israeli president Shimon Peres as a man who knew "very well how to kill." At home Erdoğan was perceived as fighting the good fight, and his personal popularity went up ten points in the opinion polls. It won him attention in the Middle East as the new champion of the Palestinian cause. The Pavlovian response was fixed. Criticizing Israel was both right in itself and earned the instant gratification of applause at home and abroad.

There followed the bizarre humiliation of the Turkish ambassador when an Israeli deputy foreign minister invited him to a meeting and made him sit on a very low chair in front of the assembled press corps. Although Israel apologized for the slight, it offered no regret for a much more serious incident in May 2010 when Israeli commandos intercepted an international flotilla that had set off very publicly to run the blockade of the Gaza Strip. Israeli commandos rappelled onto the deck of the *Mavi Marmara*, the largest vessel owned by a Turkish Islamic charity, which had set out with the tacit approval of authorities if not actual encouragement. During the course of the assault, nine activists were killed, including a nineteen-year-old with dual American and Turkish citizenship. Ankara demanded a formal apology and compensation for the bereaved families.

It was a chastening incident for both sides. The Turkish government was in the awkward position of having to restrain its own public opinion, which believed it had underreacted to the assault. The UN Human Rights Council concluded that "the conduct of the Israeli military and other personnel towards the flotilla passengers was not only disproportional to the occasion but demonstrated levels of totally unnecessary and incredible violence."[9] The less-charitable view in Western capitals was that the Turkish government had botched an exercise of soft power and, through fault or design, let itself be used in an unnecessary escalation of an already tense situation.

The *Mavi Marmara* incident only added to Turkey's standing in the "emerging" Arab world weary of the hypocrisy of the old regimes. However, it also left Ankara vulnerable to the same accusations of double standards it once leveled against others. It defended the rights of the people of the Gaza Strip yet turned a blind eye to far greater atrocities in Southern Sudan because of the commercial importance Turkey invested in Khartoum. "It is not possible for a Muslim to commit genocide," Erdoğan said in defense of a visit by Sudanese president Omar al-Bashir, who faced charges of war crimes in the International Criminal Court in The Hague.[10]

While in 2011 Turkey was happy to urge Egyptian president Hosni Mubarak to pack his bags, it was initially reticent to criticize the Libyan leader Muammar Gaddafi in order not to jeopardize lucrative business in a country where Turkish construction firms were heavily engaged. That Ankara conducts its foreign policy pragmatically, with one eye on public opinion and the other on commercial interests, should not come as a dramatic surprise.

However, the real problem is that it has not been an easy matter to calculate those best interests, particularly in the aftermath of the Arab Spring. A second UN report,[11] attempting to adjudicate in the *Mavi Marmara* incident, appeared to undermine Turkey's deep sense of indignation. While it called upon Israel to show regret, the report did not demand an admission of guilt in the form of an apology nor did it support Ankara's insistence that the embargo of Gaza violated international law. The Turkish government felt forced to go on the offensive, not simply rejecting the report but downgrading diplomatic relations with Israel, even threatening to use gun ships to run the Gaza blockade and to police offshore drilling in the Republic of Cyprus. In the 1980s Ankara, feeling isolated internationally under martial law, tried to cultivate approval in the Arab world by downgrading relations with Israel. Now the suspicion is that Ankara is trying to curry favor among the emerging actors of the Arab Spring by trying to further isolate Israel over the legitimacy of the Gaza blockade.

The Turkish response to charges that it is behaving opportunistically is one of overwhelming resentment that Israel torpedoed Turkey's efforts to bring about peace in the Middle East. It believes that its tough stance toward Israel is in the West's best interests and that the United States and Europe have been forced to be overindulgent because of their own public opinion.

What are Turkey's relations with the European Union?

Turkey is a candidate nation to join the European Union and is engaged in the complex process of harmonizing its laws and procedures to European norms. It acquired candidate status at the end of 2004 after years of lobbying, a great deal of hard bargaining, and a process of root-and-branch reform. Negotiations began the following year, though "negotiations" is something of a misnomer, since it is up to the candidate country to adopt the 80,000 pages (at last count) of EU *acquis* or law. These are divided into thirty-five chapters, covering a wide range of issues—from competition policy to food safety to financial control. Any suggestion that this is purely a technical process is belied by the large amount of political will needed by both sides for the accession process to conclude successfully.

When Turkey became a full candidate, headline-writers hailed the moment as having the same epochal importance of the collapse of the Soviet Union. It was a reward for Turkish persistence and proof of its ability to take its place in the highest councils of the developed world. Europe, though less exuberant, recognized the importance of cementing a relationship with an important ally and trading partner whose prosperity and security are intrinsic to its well-being. The European left, in particular, saw the ability to integrate a Muslim-majority nation in a post-9/11 world as evidence of the concert, not clash, of civilizations.

However, the actual course of negotiations has turned into a grueling test of each side's commitment. In the case of Turkey, accession means engaging in a process of at times controversial reform, airing a whole history of dirty linen in front of an EU public, and implementing a series of measures, from environmental protection legislation to minority rights to greater transparency over government tenures for contracts—all of which come at an economic and political cost. In the case of Europe, accession means sharing sovereignty with a populous nation that one day might claim the largest number of seats in the European Parliament and confronting the fears of the culturally introverted parts of Europe that Turkey at some fundamental level does not share European values.

The danger is that the EU negotiation process, instead of becoming a series of milestones on the way to political convergence, has become a path strewn with landmines, alienating Turkish opinion from Europe, which, it is convinced, has no intention of ever accepting Turkey as an equal.

The first thing to grasp is just how long the saga has been going on. Although commentators sometimes speak

of "enlargement fatigue," in the case of Turkey "narco-
lepsy" might be more appropriate. Ankara applied for
associate membership of what was popularly called the
Common Markets in 1959, and in 1963 it signed the Ankara
Agreement, which envisaged eventual Turkish membership should it meet the entrance criteria. However, Turkey
famously declined to grasp the opportunity when it failed
to submit in 1974 an application, in parallel with Greece,
which had thrown off the yoke of military rule. "They are the
partners [a Turkish pun on the word "common"] and we are
the market" was the slogan that reflected Turkey's fear that
the trading bloc's true intention was to swamp young and
heavily protected Turkish industries with goods of its own.
The irony was that Greece was admitted as an EU member in
1981, a year after Turkey itself suffered a military coup.

In 1987 the government of Turgut Özal put the European
Union back on Turkey's agenda, reviving Turkey's application
at a time when there was no realistic hope of being accepted.
In 1989 Turkey's eligibility was confirmed (Morocco's was
rejected), but Ankara was given the task of first completing
a Customs Union on manufactured goods that the Ankara
Agreement had envisaged. This came into play in 1996 and
essentially gave European manufactures the same unfettered
access that Turkey already enjoyed in Europe, and it made
Turkey part of the same economic zone. So while approval of
a Customs Union was clearly in Europe's economic interest,
the vote in the European Parliament was a close-run thing,
as many European MPs saw it, rightly, as a step toward
membership.

With the implementation of a Customs Union, Ankara
could justifiably argue that its economy was better integrated into Europe than the new wave of former Warsaw

Pact candidates, which were then overtaking it in the admissions queue. With the notable exception of agricultural goods and the free movement of labor, the Customs Union meant that Turkey had succeeded in entering the Common Markets to which it had sought membership all those years before. Roughly half of Turkish trade is with the European Union, and Europe is an important source of much-coveted foreign direct investment (FDI) into Turkey. However, Europe had moved on to become a political union. Already by 1992 the Maastricht Treaty had drawn up the framework for tighter European integration, including a single currency, and the Lisbon Treaty (2009) set out a common EU foreign and defense policy.

This, of course, is the problem. As long as Turkey is not a full member, it remains outside decision-making councils, even those affecting the Customs Union. Turkey must implement the EU tariff regime over which it has no say, meaning that its trade, be it with China, Nigeria, or Brazil, is regulated in Brussels. On the very important matter of defense, the shoe is on the other foot. Turkey as a full member of NATO has been reluctant to see NATO resources and military assets transferred to an EU-administered body in which it has no say. Its objections became an important obstacle to the development of a European Defense and Security Policy (EDSP) distinct from NATO. The issue is further complicated because Cyprus (which is a member of the EDSP but not of NATO) is excluded from any joint council or NATO's Partnership for Peace because of Turkish objections.

The European Union's negotiations coincided with Turkey's emergence from a major economic crisis, and the prospect of membership provided what analysts at the time described as an "anchor," an assurance to the foreign investment community that it was following a roadmap toward institutional reform. Since 2004 Turkey has indeed become far more prosperous, having broken the back of a vicious cycle of debt (having to pay more to borrow less) that now afflicts some European countries themselves. Indeed, as emerging markets in general began to acquire a greater weight in the world economy and as the euro wobbled in currency markets, voices in Turkey began to question whether the European bloc represents a secure future. They posit Russia, Ukraine, or even Iran as the important markets of the years ahead. Others doubt this vision and believe that European society provides a model of "jam today" rather than illusive "jam tomorrow."

This debate has attracted the attention of the United States, eager to secure Turkey to European institutions. As mentioned earlier, the United States has remained one of the strongest advocates of Turkish entry—a stand that sometimes raises eyebrows in Brussels itself. In 1995 the Labor Party's then opposition leader Tony Blair's first policy decision was, at U.S. behest, to use his party's influence in the European parliament to pass the Customs Union. In 2010, then defense secretary Robert Gates publicly attributed an unreliable tendency in Turkish foreign policy to the failure of Brussels to give Turkey a clear membership perspective.

Official Turkish policy is that EU membership remains an essential priority, and that cultivating ties beyond Europe makes Turkey more, not less, valuable to its future partners. "Turkey can walk and chew gum at the same time," is how Egemen Bağış, appointed Turkey's chief negotiator to the European UNION in 2009, describes Turkey's multidimensional foreign policy. However, this may not be strictly true. Turkey's higher profile in world affairs is not incidental to its status as an EU applicant country but a direct consequence. Turkish public opinion often sees America or the Arab world competing with the European Union for Turkey's attention when the reality is that Turkey is the more valued ally if it is a part of Europe. It may be necessary for domestic consumption to paint membership as one option among many and it might be a good negotiating tactic. Yet for Ankara to believe its own rhetoric and take its eye off the ball of full membership would be a historic error.

Is Turkey really European enough to be a member of the EU?

"Welcome to Asia," reads the sign at the exit of Istanbul's Bosporus Bridge and it is true that only Turkish Thrace, about 3 percent of the country's total land mass, is actually part of the European continent. On the other hand, the other 97 percent has been an intrinsic part of the history of Europe for at least as long as Herodotus thought of Europe in terms of political geography. The Ottoman Empire was very much a Balkan power, even before the capture of Constantinople in 1453. It is fanciful to think of the Ottomans as a Muslim empire engaged in permanent jihad with the West, when the underlying reality is that from the inception of the empire to World War I, the princes of Europe allied themselves with the sultan to fight one another. There was never a time when the "Porte" (the term synonymous with the Ottoman government) was outside the equation of European power politics. It was part of the Concert of Europe in the nineteenth century, and while Czar Nicholas I may not have actually been the first to coin the phrase "sick man of Europe" to describe the Ottoman Empire, the expression caught on. It was never the sick man of Asia Minor.

Given that the whole Atatürk agenda was to emulate European institutions to catch up with the West and allow Turks to fit seamlessly into the modern world, there is no reason why Europe should come to a juddering halt at the toll booths on the Asian side of the Bosphorus Bridge. Much of the enthusiasm for EU membership comes from mid-sized Turkish cities, like Gaziantep, located near the Syrian border, where factory managers follow the fine print of EU standards and regulations every bit as closely as their competitors in Portugal or Poland. A supranational European identity also presents the prospect of a political resolution for Turkey's Kurds in the way that it did in conflicts in Northern Ireland and the Basque region of Spain. Liberal-minded Turks see the European Union as providing a framework for the country to contain the excesses of ultranationalist or doctrinaire Islamist politics.

Engaging in an accession process is not something the European Commission takes lightly, and clearly it would not have pressed the start button were it not convinced of the merits of Turkey's case. However, it is an understatement to say not all of Europe is convinced of the merits of further enlargement. If Europe is defined in terms of its Christian heritage (as the Vatican tried to insist, during the drafting of the abortive European Constitution), this would logically exclude Muslim Turkey. There are those who argue that Turkey is simply not part of a European value system. Evidence of this is the reluctance of Turkish migrants in Europe to assimilate into their host nations. Others point to attitudes toward women, the most extreme example of which are premeditated "honor" killings of women who defy the sexual mores of their community. In the post-9/11 trauma, there are those who see public manifestations of

Islam—mosque building or headscarves—as political statements and potentially threatening.

Even those who do not feel strongly about these issues sometimes wonder why Europe should go out on a limb to court Turkey. The 1991 Gulf War brought home to the Brussels community the fact that accepting Turkey as part of Europe also meant accepting that Europe now had a border with Iran, Syria, and Iraq.

Of course, Europe has never defined itself as a Christian union, and to keep Turkey out on religious grounds would be to label as second-class citizens the more than 16 million Muslim (estimated by the Zentral-Institut Islam-Archiv-Deutschland) already living in the European Union. If some Turks have failed to integrate into European countries—and of course the picture is far more complex than an anti-immigrant lobby would paint—it is equally a black mark against attitudes and policies of the societies in which they live. Until recently it was easier for a German-speaker born in Kazakhstan to become a German citizen than a third-generation ethnic Turk born in Hamburg.

And if one thinks of honor killings as a form of domestic violence, this, unhappily, would not differentiate Turkey from the rest of Europe. Violence in the home is the primary cause of injury and death among European women aged 16 to 44. In Germany, almost 300 women a year are killed by men with whom they used to live. In France that figure is one death every three days. According to a report from the Council of Europe, "the incidence of domestic violence seems to increase with income and level of education."[12] It does not argue these grim statistics are the product of Western values.

Turkey's human rights record is also much criticized and there are those who despair at Ankara's wavering commitment to raising its game to root out undemocratic practices. By the same token, it is the European left—Greens and Liberals—who are most enthusiastic about Turkish membership, pointing to the incremental reforms that Turkey has undertaken to keep its membership application on track. Many Turks, too, believe that external pressure from the European Union is the most effective engine of reform.

At the same time, there is a significant body of opinion which sees the EU process as a humiliating gauntlet that Turkey is being made to run. In 2005 Prime Minister Erdoğan tried to reconcile the two camps and, in an address to the Azerbaijani Parliament, said there was "no turning back" for Turkey on the road to European integration, turning the cliché of "Copenhagen Criteria" for EU membership into the "Ankara criteria"—that is, a self-motivating process.

If one thinks of identity as defined by overlapping and concentric circles—from the God you worship to the football team you support—then "European" might not be the label uppermost in most Turks' minds. Some feel spurned by European attitudes and remind themselves of competing loyalties, which include an abstract cultural affinity with Central Asia or religious affinities with the Islamic world.

On the other hand, millions of Turks do consider themselves European for the excellent reason that they trace their ancestry to the European reaches of the empire, many of whom fled as refugees during the Balkan Wars of the late nineteenth and early twentieth centuries. Some 500,000 Turks were expatriated from Greece in the exchange of population decreed by the Treaty of Lausanne (1923). As late as 1989, 300,000 Bulgarian Turks fled to Turkey from a campaign of forced assimilation, some of whom have remained or retained close ties. A third of geographical Europe was once part of the Ottoman Empire, including five EU member states (Rumania, Bulgaria, Cyprus, Hungary, Greece) and seven potential candidates. As a result, there are neighborhoods in and around Istanbul called "New Bosnia" or the "Albanian Village" and there are families throughout Turkey whose last names refer to their grandparents' hometowns in cities that are now part of the European Union.

Apart from proud disdain, the Turkish response to the assertion they are not European enough to be part of the European Union (after recollecting that not a square inch of EU-member Cyprus is in geographic Europe) is that it is too late to change the rules of the game. The 1963 Ankara Agreement recognizes Turkey as a European nation and allows for eventual membership. *Pacta sunt servanda*— "treaties are to be obligated," not just Turks but many Europeans themselves would argue. Turkey points to its role as a founder member of the Organization for Security and Cooperation in Europe and the (non-EU) Council of Europe, which administers the European Court of Human Rights. Turkish football teams not only play in European championships, but an Istanbul side Galatasaray beat Arsenal in 2000 to win the UEFA cup. And if that is not proof enough of its European credentials, a Turkish pop star, Sertap Erener, won the Eurovision Song Contest in 2003 with a very Euro-pop ditty called "Every Way That I Can."

Nonetheless, it might be useful to explore the logic behind Turkey's application to become part of the European Union.

Turkey is just too big a country for Europe to ignore. Turkey is already Europe's fifth-largest export market, and those in favor of Turkish entry are eager to stress the win-win of incorporating a fertile market for goods and financial services contiguous to Europe's boundaries. Cooperation with NATO-member Turkey is important for European security as well as for Europe's ability to control the traffic in drugs and illegal migrants that pass through Turkey.

Turkish figures put the number of Turks living in Europe at 3.1 million, but estimates of ethnic Turks with European citizenship suggest that figure is much higher—possibly five million (the population of Denmark). This means that in countries like Germany, where there is now a third generation and even a fourth generation in the wake of the flux of a Turkish and ethnic Kurdish workforce, what happens in Turkey is very much an issue of domestic politics. Turkish nationalists may argue that the EU admission process is an attempt to achieve by stealth what the Great Powers failed to achieve by might—an undermining of Turkish sovereignty. By contrast, the view that dominates the European Commission is that Brussels has everything to gain from a stable, prosperous Turkey and much to lose from one that is volatile and outside Europe's ambit.

Europe needs Turkey and vice versa. Unfortunately (as it demonstrated during the breakup of Yugoslavia), having a unified foreign policy is not what Europe does best. The one strategy it has successfully pursued is that of enlargement—a process of "voluntary regime change" that rewarded Spain, Portugal, and Greece for shaking off dictatorship and that was instrumental in shaping the destinies of the once-Soviet-controlled countries of Eastern and Central Europe. It is a process that Brussels is now contemplating for Serbia and even Iceland. Croatia's candidacy is well advanced.

However, Europe eyes Turkey the way a boa constrictor does a rhinoceros—it could be the one political entity it might not be able to digest. The United Kingdom, among the most enthusiastic of Turkey's backers, is suspected of embracing so unwieldy an applicant nation because it would forever scupper the notion of a federal and politically cohesive Europe, something it fears and loathes. Independently of Turkish membership, Europe has realized that it moves at the speed of its weakest member. The perilous state of the Greek economy produced a crisis in the viability of a single currency eurozone. Monetary union is only operable where it can be reinforced by a federal economic policy. This has led to speculation that Europe may itself be forced to regroup into different tiers of membership or one that allows different states to opt out of some commitments. This à la carte Europe would, paradoxically, work in Turkey's favor.

While Turkey sees its youthful population as an asset to a Europe in which the workforce will struggle to support an aging population, conservative European opinion and their political champions see a tide of new Islamic immigration that could overwhelm its own institutions and values. Despite its newfound prosperity, Turkey is still poor relative to the rest of Europe, and there are, as we have seen, destabilizing regional imbalances within Turkey itself. Not even the most optimistic forecaster believes that Turkey will join the European Union tomorrow or even in five years' time. It can only do so when its own society and economy are on a relatively equal footing with that of Europe and will not shed population.

Selling Turkey to a European electorate remains far more difficult than was the case for previous rounds of enlargement. At the level of political rhetoric, Central and Eastern Europe were not so much allowed into Europe as welcomed back. They were prodigals returning home, admitted through a purging of their communist past. Spain, Greece, and Portugal were rewarded for discarding their dictatorships. Prague,

Budapest, and of course Berlin reassumed their place in European cultural life. Turkey, by contrast, has been on a slow journey of incremental reform.

To many in Europe, the decision to negotiate with Turkey is at best a practical decision—to expand the European market and secure an ally. No walls will fall; there will be no color-coded revolution. It is process without catharsis. Indeed, the argument of the German Greens, for example, is not just that Turkey will change but that Turkey will force a change within Europe itself and oblige a blinkered continent finally to come to terms with its cultural diversity. This is a challenge that a union founded to bring peace to postwar Germany and France should take in its stride, but one that conservative sections of European society have been reluctant to accept. In this sense Turkey has an advantage. It is a society that knows it must change.

Will Turkey successfully conclude negotiations (and what about Cyprus)?

This really is rocket science, because one has to calculate whether a fast-changing Turkey will finally connect with a Europe whose institutional shape in ten or fifteen years will be very different from today. Precedent is on the side of Turkey getting in. Europe has expanded from a core of six nations to a gaggle of twenty-seven after five rounds of enlargements between 1973 and 2007. Norway decided through popular referendum not to join, and Greenland opted out when it seceded from Denmark, but no country which has started negotiations has failed to finish. This has not stopped many from openly speculating that Turkey will prove the exception to this rule.

It sometimes appears as if Ankara was more concerned about becoming a full candidate to the European Union than in getting on with the hard slog of becoming a full member. There is a certain logic to this. Once Turkey signed on to the accession process, foreign investors began to view the country with greater interest. Direct foreign investment shot up. Actual accession would mean taking on expensive social legislation. Turkish history books devote so much time to describing how difficult it was to win sovereignty from Europe in 1923 that the population may be ill-prepared for sharing it. Turkey's friends in Europe—and these include Britain, Italy, and Spain as well as many of the new accession states—wonder why Turkey doesn't make life easier for them by, for example, repealing articles of the penal code, which make it an offense to insult Turkishness and malign state institutions, and also restrictions on freedoms of expression through laws under which many prominent intellectuals, journalists, even the author of this book, were once tried.

However, the Turkish public, not to mention the bureaucrats doing the actual negotiations, believe that it is Europe which is putting obstacles in Turkey's way. Conservative politicians in France, Germany, and Austria would like to fob Turkey off with what they refer to as a "privileged partnership." How such a partnership would operate is not readily defined but, in any case, is vigorously opposed by Ankara, which suspects it would continue to give Turkey obligations of membership with none of the decision-making powers. This means that Turkey might have to wait out a generation of naysaying European politicians, and Turkish politicians are themselves not famous for looking beyond the next bend. Public opinion in Turkey tends to focus on the bad news and support for membership is in fast decline.

This is far from unusual for accession countries, and enthusiasm would likely return once entry became a realistic proposition. Turkish public opinion suffers from the reverse of Groucho Syndrome. It wants to join a club that wants them as a member and resents one which does not.

An immediate confidence-building measure would be to change the system that forces Turks to go through a lengthy and humiliating procedure to get what is called a "Schengen visa" to continental Europe or to visit the United Kingdom. This process can entail showing the deeds to a house and details of bank accounts. Not even noncandidates Serbia and Albania face such restrictions. To end this visa regime Turkey must make facility for repatriation of its citizens residing in Europe illegally, as well as accept the return of third-party nationals who enter Europe illegally via Turkey.

However, the issue deemed by many commentators to be the stumbling block is that of Cyprus, still divided since 1974, when an attempt backed by the junta in Greece to force union with the mainland was countered by a military invasion from Turkey. Turkey is alone in recognizing the breakaway Republic of Northern Cyprus, which slipped into existence in 1983 by declaring itself—one week after the election that ended martial law on the Turkish mainland and before the new Özal government could be formed. Turkey has supported the partition both financially and militarily for reasons to do with its own security as well as from an emotional commitment to protect the Turkish community from intercommunal violence. In a second stage of the invasion, Turkish troops occupied over a third of the island and, contrary to UN resolutions, some 150,000 Turkish mainlanders were encouraged to migrate to Turkish-controlled Cyprus. Their presence is resented not just by Greek Cypriots but increasingly by

Turkish Cypriots, who feel they are becoming a minority in their own homeland.

For years, and at a great opportunity cost to itself, Turkey resisted international pressure and supported a Northern Cypriot hard line. Finally, in 2004, Turkey worked seriously with UN Secretary General Kofi Annan to broker a settlement. The Annan Plan was accepted in referendum in Northern Cyprus but overwhelmingly rejected in the south. Turkey blames the European Union for accepting Cyprus as a member despite this rejection, thereby importing a conflict into the European Union, one that colors the European Union's perception of Turkey. The Acquis Communautaire is suspended for the Turkish north. Ankara does not recognize the Republic of Cyprus but, more to the point, has not extended the Customs Union to Cyprus (in the form of implementing the Additional Protocol of the Association Agreement, as it was committed to doing after it became an accession candidate). In fact, Turkish ports have been closed to Republic of Cyprus vessels since 1994 in retaliation against the ban on Turkish Cypriot exports to the European Union imposed by the European Court of Justice.

In July 2012 the Republic of Cyprus will assume the six-month presidency of the European Union, and this puts Ankara in the position of engaging in negotiations led by a country it does not recognize. It has already announced it will suspend the process. If this were not crisis enough, Turkey now objects to a maritime agreement between Cyprus and Israel that would divvy the huge reserves of gas and oil in the Eastern Mediterranean basin. It does so on grounds that this ignores the interests of Northern Cyprus. Its warnings coincide with brinkmanship with Israel and Turkish promises to patrol the Eastern Mediterranean to allow humanitarian relief to penetrate the Israeli naval blockade of Gaza.

The issue is further complicated by the fact that it is a U.S. company, Noble Energy, which is conducting the energy exploration and extraction.

The immediate result is that eight Acquis negotiating chapters referring to the Customs Union will remain frozen and that no chapter can be formally closed until Turkey lifts its embargo. Ankara again accuses Turco-sceptics within the European Union of hiding behind the skirts of the Cyprus issue. France, for one, openly opposes the opening of another four chapters, which would preclude an alternative to full membership. Those in Turkey who are opposed to the whole European project, either out of nationalism or out of a suspicion of globalization, who are opposed to the whole European project to seize upon European Turco-scepticism as a reason to drag their feet.

However, one critical fact suggests that talks might just end in full accession. No one can say "no." No European leader, not even the French president, wants to take responsibility for actually breaking off negotiations; such a decision requires a majority vote in the EU parliament. Moreover, no group within Turkish society wants to take responsibility for ending the European dream. Even the far right in Turkey, which sees Europe as the enemy, says it would love to be a member but that the treacherous Europeans will only string Turkey along and never accede.

So here is a risky prediction—one I confess in which I become less confident over time. The wheels of the Turkish accession process will turn very slowly but only in one direction, and in the end Ankara will be offered full membership. Some in Europe believe the surprise punch-line will be that Turkey down the road will feel sufficiently sure of itself that, like Norway, it will then turn around and say, "Thanks, but no thanks." That, I speculate too, may be wishful thinking.

5

POLITICS ... AND THE MILITARY

What sort of political system does Turkey have?

In order to even begin membership negotiations with the
European Union, Turkey, like other candidates, had to
demonstrate that its economy was capable of integrating
with the free markets of the member states and that its political and social institutions were similarly compatible. Fine
tuning occurs during the accession process, but a nation
not committed to normative EU standards of democracy
and human rights does not get its foot in the door. These
benchmarks—referred to as the "Copenhagen Criteria" after
the location of the summit where they were agreed—are
onerous. The United States, for example, would stumble
(apart from the fact that it is not in Europe) on the stipulation
that it abolish capital punishment.

That Turkey was deemed eligible in 2004 to begin negotiations, then, lends credence that it is a democracy governed
by respect for the integrity of the ballot, parliamentary
procedure, international convention, and the rule of law.
A free electoral process has played the key role in Turkish
politics since 1950. That was the year when Turkey set a
precedent among other emerging nations by voting out the

Republican People's Party (CHP) founded by Atatürk. To compare: In Mexico, a country that political scientists once likened to Turkey, the party of the revolution—the Partido Revolucionario Institucional (PRI)—surrendered the presidency in a 2000 poll. Kim Dae-jung was elected president of South Korea only in 1997—a similar transfer of power through the ballot. Today Turkey is sometimes pushed to the front of the room as an example of how a contemporary Muslim-majority society can be democratic. Not all that long ago, it was held up as an example of how a developing society could evolve democratic institutions.

Politics are a passion in Turkey, and if the all-night talk shows and huge rallies at election time are any indication, there is little public apathy. Elections are fiercely fought under a fiendishly complicated system of proportional representation, weighted in favor of the party that scores the most in any one constituency. This is designed to be fair and yet still produce strong, single-party government; it is possible to produce a majority with less than 35 percent of the vote. It was a sign of how fractured politics were in the 1990s that even such a system could only produce coalitions.

What is less fair is that the system discriminates against parties that fail to cross a 10-percent threshold of the national vote. This effectively keeps regionally based (read "Kurdish") parties from getting into parliament unless deputies stand as independents or in an electoral pact with another party. For example, in the 2002 election, the Justice and Development (AK) Party won two-thirds of the 550 seats in parliament with only 34 percent of the vote; the opposition CHP won a third of the seats with 19 percent (there were a few independents as well). This means that some 45 percent of the voters had nothing to show for their ballots, as they supported parties that failed to get across the 10-percent threshold. Of course, other electoral systems, including Great Britain's single-member constituencies, notoriously "waste" votes, as does any majority-vote presidential system. By contrast, a system of perfect representation (like the Israeli) produces multi-party coalitions, which means that very small parties have disproportionately large bargaining power. Paradoxically, in subsequent elections the AK Party received fewer seats with a higher percentage of the votes. In 2011 just under 50 percent of the vote earned the party 59 percent of the seats, an indication that the electorate had learned how to vote tactically, consigning to oblivion parties they knew would not qualify for seats.

Put the question another way and ask whether Turkey is a smooth-functioning democracy and many Turks would raise their hands. Another, far less comfortable landmark in postwar Turkish politics was a military coup in 1960 that resulted in the courts hanging the elected prime minister and two of his ministers on a long list of charges involving corruption, abuses of power, and violating the constitution. That set a counterprecedent of tension—and, some might argue, an unhealthy codependency—between an elected and an unelected authority. There have been two subsequent occasions—in 1971–1973 and 1980–1983—when the military stepped in to replace the government with those of their own choosing. In 1997 the chiefs of staff successfully maneuvered to unseat the ruling coalition in what pundits waggishly referred to as Turkey's "postmodern coup."

These seizures of power have been violent shocks to the body politic and, certainly after 1971, they appeared to legitimate the systematic abuse of human rights even after the country had returned to civilian rule. Turkey has made important strides in casting off what human rights observers referred to as a "culture of impunity," in which police interrogators using implements of torture or special teams carrying out assassinations in the Kurdish southeast scarcely bothered to cover their tracks. Though there are occasional relapses, the country has largely shed its "Midnight Express" image where the citizen is defenseless against the state. At the same time, the question of where authority lies and how it can be held accountable remains one of the great conundrums of Turkish politics. The public is aware that major state institutions including the judiciary are in need of reform.

A more accurate term for the interdependence of elected and unelected authority is "administrative tutelage," which describes a situation in which the bureaucracy, including the military, is not so much the handmaiden of popularly elected government as a gatekeeper against untutored popular impulses. In Turkey, "state" and "government" are not used synonymously. Governments are formally accountable to an electorate but in practice that accountability has been circumscribed by a bureaucratic and military elite.

A benign way of putting this is that a bureaucracy tutors an elected government, which over time develops the necessary competence and expertise. For example, Turkish cities have parallel systems of administration, one run by an elected mayor, the other by an appointed governor. In some cases, responsibilities are different (the governor gets the schools and the police force; mayors run the water department and collect the trash). In other cases, like transport, they necessarily overlap. Overlapping authority, however, can be a way of avoiding accountability. The decision on whether to build a new third bridge across the Istanbul Bosphorus, one that has immense implications for the city's future, has been taken in a back office of the Highways Department in faraway Ankara. Before a feasibility or environmental impact study could be made, the government passed special legislation to relieve it of the obligation to seek permission from a planning authority. "Subsidiarity," a principle much in vogue in the European Union—the notion that decision making should devolve to the lowest feasible level—is only slowly taking root in Turkey's very centralized system. Power still rises to the top.

In an overcentralized bureaucracy, the point of contact between official and citizen could be brusque. Trying to get the gas man to come or enroll a child for school used to mean looking for an inside contact, a bit of influence, or someone to bribe. Nowadays, you take a number at the door or make an appointment online, and it sometimes takes a while to get used to the idea that the system works. It doesn't work everywhere, of course (Transparency International rated Turkey 56th out of 178 countries in 2010, higher than Slovakia but worse than South Africa). A more cynical way of looking at "tutelage" is as an uneasy alliance between state and government—the state retains its prerogatives to exercise power and define core political values, while government is free to get on with the business of rewarding their supporters. The political system lacks maturity, and many Turks view politics as less about ideology or public policy than about patronage. This lack of trust tends to reinforce a lack of responsibility, with politicians making hay (or at least raking in the spoils) while the fiscal sun shines.

A surprisingly large number of people trust in the military as the ultimate guarantor of the integrity of the system. Certainly in the past, politicians behaved as if they expected a military intervention to rescue them from their own reck-lessness. Such expectations have become anachronistic, and one theme of modern Turkish politics is the effort to "demili-tarize" public life.

The most blatant example of administrative tutelage has been that which the military attempted to exert over elected officials. The Turkish word for "memorandum" evokes March 12, 1971, when the chiefs of staff issued an ultimatum to the government to step aside in favor of one that could deal with public disorder. Again in 2007, with the dawning of the electronic age, the military posted on their website a warning about the course of the coming presidential elec-tion. In 1971, the government resigned. In 2007, on the other hand, the government stood its ground and renewed its mandate at the ballot box. Something had changed in the interim.

The military is not the only source of tutelage. High court judges often behave as civil servants with an eye more to raisons d'état than jurisprudence. The highest judicial body in the land, the Constitutional Court, for example, has taken the decision to ban some twenty-seven political parties. These have been parties either to the left or the religious right or those that advocate Kurdish nationalism. Parties with real popular support have resurfaced almost immedi-ately under another name, only to face yet again court action. The most notorious of recent closure cases was in 2008 when the Constitutional Court heard a case to shut down the governing AK Party for violating the secular nature of the Turkish state—even though it had just been elected with an even larger percentage of the popular vote. In the final verdict the court stopped short of closing the party, issuing a financial penalty instead.

Political parties could make a better case against state authoritarianism were they themselves not so hierarchical. It is the central party, not constituencies, that decide which candidates stand where on the electoral list—a system that ensures obedience. Alternative factions are as likely to split away and form parties of their own rather than challenge the leadership who enjoy what is popularly called a "sultanic reign" over their party. Leaders manage to stay at the head of the party even after they lose an election, which makes it almost impossible for the party to regroup, bring in fresh blood, and redirect its message to appeal to the electorate. In recent years, the ineffectiveness of opposition has been the weak link in the political system and has fueled the arrogance of the party in power. Deniz Baykal served as a minister as far back as 1974 when the government installed him as leader of the Republican People's Party (CHP), where he remained in opposition for over a decade, despite losing three general elections in a row. (In May 2010 he was eventually dethroned, not by party delegates at a conference but because of a leaked video that caught him in flagrante delicto with his secretary, whom he had made an MP.) Like charismatic sects, many of the parties associated with figures of post-1960 coup politics—Turgut Özal, Süleyman Demirel, Bülent Ecevit—have disappeared or shriveled to irrelevancy once their leaders were gone.

On top of that, people often refer to a "deep state"—an unseen inner circle, which by fair means but often foul ensures that the elected politicians stay within well-defined parameters. This is not just a form of paranoia (even conspiracy theorists have enemies). Turkey has a history of covert operations organized by an entrenched old guard who have manipulated ultranationalist gangs to get rid of Kurdish activists or create chaos when the elected government was going in a direction of which they did not approve. In 1996 a gangster, his moll, a chief of police, and a progovernment Kurdish MP were in a car that ran into a truck in the northwestern town of Susurluk, some 200 miles from Istanbul, providing evidence of links between the security forces, politics, and organized crime. In more recent times, state prosecutors have charged members of a network codenamed "Ergenekon"—which I discuss below—accusing them of plotting bloody provocations with the aim of fomenting a coup.

While political parties might be loath to acknowledge their influence, pressures from the outside world—particularly the European Union—have been powerful motors of reform. Turkey's desire to join NATO, and to be accepted into the Western alliance against the Soviet Union, provided the carrot to move to a multiparty system. However, exogenous influences have not been the only driving force. The 1980 coup and the restrictive nature of the 1982 Constitution are sometimes seen as having created a depoliticized generation. At the same time, a new sense of politics began to emerge that was no longer about "capturing" the state to further an agenda of left or right. Rather it was to transfer effective power to the networks of civil society. Women no longer made the tea at political meetings but engaged in feminist movements. A popular news magazine, such as *Nokta* (it means "period," like the French news periodical *Le Point*), which began publication in 1982, started peering behind the closed doors of everyday life, using pop sociology to reveal what really went on in schools, at work, and, of course, in the bedroom. Prisoner family associations blossomed into human rights organizations. Environmentalists banded together to try to save unique wetlands from the scourge of sugar-beet farming and or the loggerhead sea turtle from tourist development. In 1996 Turkey was host to the UN Habitat II conference, and the large nongovernmental organization component helped inspire an NGO movement within Turkey itself.

Progress has been far from uninterrupted. The Higher Education Council (YÖK), which was created under the 1982 Constitution, was forced to retreat from its original intention to administer all Turkish universities under one umbrella. The state monopoly on higher education was broken and provision was made for the endowment of private universities. However, YÖK, as well as the president of the Republic, can override decisions taken by the faculty, including the choice of deans and rectors. In general, however, the resourcefulness of civil society in Turkey is becoming an increasingly credible alternative to state tutelage.

Are Turkish political parties deeply ideological?

The terms "left" and "right" in Western politics tend to describe the state's role as a regulatory and economic agent, although even here there is "cultural blurring." Among Republicans in the United States, for example, "the state should keep its nose out of business" is a right-wing sentiment, whereas "the state should not interfere with a women's right to terminate a pregnancy" is not. Unsurprisingly, Turkish parties also define themselves in relation to their own history and political culture.

Turkey's political landscape is not always easy to negotiate by outsiders if only because political parties do not always fit into what most would regard as the conventional spectrum of left to right. It can come as a surprise, for example, to discover that the European Green parties—radicals on environmental and civil libertarian issues—feel an affinity for the reform agenda of a right-wing Islamic-leaning party, while European socialists criticize a Turkish fellow party of the Socialist International on the grounds that it is too close to the military or intolerant of Kurdish rights. Many European conservative politicians who reinforce their political message with an appeal to family and religious values feel distinctly uncomfortable with Turkish conservatives who try to do the same, using similar values but a different religion.

The watershed in Central and Eastern European politics is how to deal with the memory of the Soviet-inspired system. A similar watershed in Turkish politics was the 1950 election, when Atatürk's party was voted out of office. The seminal figure in the pantheon of the Turkish right remains Adnan Menderes, the prime minister who was hanged in 1961, along with two of his ministers, during a period of martial law. The execution endowed his successors with a perpetual sense of grievance. They see themselves as involved in a battle to clip the wings of the self-appointed guardians of the Turkish state—particularly the military—and to welcome Islamic observance and values in public life. The left fears the consequences of unchecked political power and the demagogic appeal of religion. They too have martyrs of sorts—the great poet Nâzım Hikmet, who was stripped of his citizenship and died in exile in Moscow, and the young firebrand revolutionary Deniz Gezmiş, who was hanged in 1972 along with two comrades and who came to symbolize the brutality of the military regime. The last death by execution in Turkey was in 1984, although capital punishment was not totally abolished for all crimes until twenty years later. Even so, many Turkish politicians have done time in prison, including the current prime minister who served four months (he was indicted for reading a poem that, although part of the school curriculum, was deemed to politicize religion). This only increases their street credibility. Indeed, in the 2011 elections a handful of candidates, including suspects in the Ergenkon trial and those facing charges of Kurdish separatism, fought and won seats from inside their prison cell, although contrary to the immunity from prosecution enjoyed by MPs, they were not released to take their seats in parliament.

While the British right-wing complains of the "nanny state," which suffocates individual initiative, few in Turkey complain about the paternalistic "Papa State" (*devlet baba*), a source of munificence or a rich uncle whom you finagle for a jump-start in life. Come election time, there is much snipping of ribbons of public-sector projects as if these were personal behests. Practically, the argument is less over the role of the state and levels of public spending than who gets to control what. The "unseen hand" is not that of an impartial market but rather of the one who gets to pull the strings.

Party logos play an enormous importance in political identity—a legacy of low historical rates of literacy, when voters stamped a ballot paper, and it was important to attract their attention with something catchy. The most ingenious of these was the now-defunct Justice Party, which used as its logo an iron-gray horse (*demir-kır-at* in Turkish, pronounced somewhat like "democrat"); the party was named after the party of the martyred Adnan Menderes to which it was heir. The frustration is that politics becomes a debate over symbol not policy. The most hotly contested issue in higher education is not the exam system or the attempt to raise the level of student fees (though these are issues) but whether women students can wear headscarves in class. Similarly, the most important education reform in recent history was the decision in 1997 to raise the compulsory primary school education from five grades to eight. However, public discussion of this measure rarely dwelled on the practical implications of keeping children in school for three more years. Instead, it focused on whether it would keep secondary schools, designed to train Islamic clerics, from recruiting younger children.

Turkish politics is often described as being shaped by competition between rival elites and as marking a shift in economic power away from the established capital of the coastal cities to those Anatolian Tigers, a culturally conservative generation of industrialists and entrepreneurs based in Central Anatolian cities like Kayseri, Konya, and Gaziantep. This rift is often portrayed as being part of the politics of envy that separates secularists and Islamicists. And it is certainly true that what was once a hinterland is now more prosperous and outward-looking and has more political purchase. However, this phenomenon is not new. Today's nouveau riche may be more culturally conservative than those who made their money yesterday; however, it is something of an exaggeration to see Turkey as battleground between old and new money. Turkey's most established business elites are little more than three generations old and in some cases stepped in to fill a vacuum created by the disappearance of the Ottoman Greek and Armenian commercial class. Successive political parties have cultivated ties with a distinct set of clients. Turks tend to think of those who prospered in the 1980s under the prime ministry of Turgut Özal as being the "Özal rich" as opposed to the "Demirel rich" of the 1990s. If the "Erdoğan rich" of the following decade seem more powerful, this is in part because the economy is so much bigger.

Historically, successful parties tend to be coalitions of different trends. Typical of this was the Motherland Party, which came to power in 1983. It was openly referred to as being a "holy alliance" between Turkish nationalists, a religious right, and liberal free-marketeers. Though that party is no more, those factions persist and tend to constitute the Turkish right and are also well represented in the AK Party, which has dominated Turkish politics in the 2000s.

What are the major forces in Turkish politics?

All political parties are coalitions and in Turkey are cocktails of the following ingredients:

Turkish nationalism. Nationalism in Turkey is a powerful force. It differs from mere patriotism in having a racial component. Traditionally it flourishes in the Turkish borderlands, particularly in reaction to Kurdish or Alevi communities or where there were once-large Armenian communities. The "other" in the nationalist panoply can mean the rest of the world. There are, as the name suggests, a high proportion of nationalists in the Nationalist Action Party (MHP) founded by a former colonel, Alparslan Türkeş, who participated in the 1960 military coup.

However, the party has sought to distance itself from the ultranationalist Grey Wolves, gangs where some of its cadres started their political careers. Ultranationalists were most active during the 1970s when they fought with socialists for control of new neighborhoods in major cities. Some branched out into organized crime and then subcontracted their services to National Intelligence to assassinate enemies of the state, including Kurdish activists. It is these deadly antics that are celebrated in the long-running Turkish television series *Valley of the Wolves*, which has been spun off into controversial feature films that glorify Rambo-like violence in the service of the state.

"Turks have no friends but themselves" is a nationalist adage and, some might argue, one of the nationalists' goals is to turn this into a self-fulfilling prophecy. Nationalist lawyers have helped initiate prosecutions against prominent writers, including the Nobel Prize–winning Orhan Pamuk, on charges of "insulting the Turkish state" with the specific aim of alienating Turkey from European public opinion. Sadly typical was the conduct of one MHP minister of health who at the time of the great 1999 Izmit Earthquake said that Turkey had no need of outside assistance. When this proved tragically wrong—largely because of the scale of the disaster but also because the health service and the Red Crescent organization were packed with party cronies—he then turned down help from Armenia and, warned victims from accepting "tainted" blood from Greece. On that particular occasion the MHP badly misjudged the mood of the nation, which was touched by outside concern. However, the, nationalist tenets—including the depiction of Kurdishness as a threat to the unitary state, as well as the belief that Western powers have an ulterior strategy to divide and weaken Turkey—have found a comfortable place in the political mainstream. While some commentators watch the rise of pro-Islamic politics in Turkey with ill-concealed horror, they may be overlooking the really scary ones on the block.

The religious right. Islamist party politics in Turkey did not start in the mosque but in rivalry for control of the Union of Chambers and Commodity Exchanges, which in the 1960s had the all-important function of allocating foreign exchange for imports. Necmettin Erbakan (1926–2011), the general secretary of that organization, was in fact a German-trained engineer who helped design parts for the Leopard tank, a German tank first introduced in 1965. He formed his own party—the National Salvation Party—when he found his path blocked in Turkey's established parties. His "National View" platform was a mix of social justice, economic self-sufficiency, and a call for a more prominent place in public life for Sunni Islam. This message found a welcome echo among some Turkish workers in German whose experience of discrimination fueled anti-Western and anti-European resentment. Another powerful base included those who had business interests in Saudi Arabia and who believed that Turkey should expand commercial ties in the Middle East, where it had a cultural affinity.

In order to escape the constitutional prohibition of mixing religion and politics, Erbakan developed a coded language and style of dress that told his supporters—but not the public prosecutor—where his sympathies lay. Male supporters of his party often wore a "chin strap" beard and the women a headscarf that concealed their hair. The National Salvation Party took part in coalition governments in the 1970s and Erbakan became prime minister when his Welfare Party came first in the 1995 election, albeit with 21 percent of the vote.

The center (liberal) right. Members of the center right resemble the European and American right and are free market–oriented and probusiness. Many are Western-educated either abroad or in the many Western-language schools in Turkey.

The Turkish left. The Turkish left is an equally broad spectrum, replete with a "socialism in one country" nationalist-Stalinist fringe. Today the left-wing mantle is borne by the

Republican People's Party (CHP), the founding party of the Republic, and therefore it claims the legitimacy of its association with Atatürk. Historically, the CHP, by being dismissive of right-wing populism, projected an elitist image that circumscribed its electoral appeal. In 1972 Bülent Ecevit, a minister for labor and a fiery orator, managed to reorientate the CHP to a position left of center and spoke to the demands of the new migrants to the city. Ecevit split off from his old party after the 1980 coup and was uncompromising in his rejection of Kurdish nationalism. As leader of the Democratic Left Party (DSP), he returned to the prime ministry in 1999 (twenty years after holding the post as head of the CHP) at the head of a coalition with right-wing parties. It was that government which steered Turkey into the 2001 economic crisis. However, it was progressive in that it continued to legislate reforms aimed at moving Turkey toward EU accession.

In recent years, the CHP became less inclusive and more committed to defending the values of secularism against encroachment from the religious right. This led to accusations that it openly sympathized with the military's intent to confront a democratically elected government. It remained protectionist and antiglobalist at a time when the British Labour Party was becoming New Labour. It is only now, under new leadership, that it has begun to rethink its message. However the party continues to tug in opposing directions—it is the advocate of organized labor and the traditional left but also the ideological home of the bureaucratic elite.

The CHP has a strong geographical base, drawing its support from the coastal regions, where people enjoy a more cosmopolitan and Western lifestyle. It also has a religious component and tends to attract the support of Turkey's large Alevi community, Alevi being a variant of Shi'ite Islam who make up at least 15 percent of the population. The Alevis ally themselves with the CHP out of a suspicion of the conservative and religious right, which tends to regard their lax, more humanistic beliefs as heterodox and which pressures them to conform to the mainstream.

The Kurdish left. The Peace and Democracy Party (BDP) is the current incarnation of the Kurdish nationalist party in Turkey, its predecessors periodically shut down by the Constitutional Court. It does not see itself in conflict with the outlawed Kurdistan Workers Party (PKK), and in that sense it is fair to call it the PKK's political wing. It understands rather than denounces the use of violence. At the same time, it adopts a program intended to appeal to the civil libertarian mainstream of Turkish politics. Despite the conservative nature of Kurdish society, the BDP and its predecessors are probably the least homophobic and most outspoken on gender equality of the political parties.

Turkish liberals. Those who hold out against the polarization are the homeless persons of Turkish politics. Many who supported the AK Party's reformist drive to get into the European Union continue to back its fight against the military and support the attempt to produce a more civil-libertarian constitution. Some liberals have been welcomed into the party as AK Party MPs, and it would be an exaggeration to say they are simply there as window dressing. However, the AK Party's need to attend to its conservative base means that their influence is limited. The growing authoritarianism of the AKP leadership, fueled by a general lack of accountability in the system, has been the cause of some disillusionment. At the same time, the CHP, damaged by in-fighting, and with the "statist" faction getting the upper hand, has proven an equally unreliable host.

How active is the Turkish press?

Freedom House, the Washington-based think tank that hands out grades to countries according to the state of their civil liberties and political rights, scratches its head in perplexity when it comes to Turkey. The picture is a confusing mix, "an ever-shifting dichotomy between democratic progress and resistance to reform."[1] Nowhere is that confusion more apparent than when it comes to the country's media. The Turkish press is varied and vocal, and at the same time restricted.

At least Turks cannot claim to be badly informed. There are some thirty-five national newspaper titles, though total circulation remains low for a country of its size—4.5 million or the equivalent of one London or New York tabloid. There are more than two dozen dedicated news channels, both terrestrial and cable. This is in addition to a large number of low-budget provincial city channels as well as innumerable private radio stations. There are also well-established Internet news portals. Rival cable and satellite platforms broadcast foreign news and special interest programs. Chat rooms hum and many politicians, even the president (@cbabdullahgul), feels obliged to Tweet.

Turkish Television and Radio (TRT), the public broadcast corporation, operates multiple domestic channels, dedicated Kurdish- and Arabic-language stations, and a Turkish-language station that broadcasts around the globe. The first challenge to TRT's monopoly came in 1990 from a pirate station that took advantage of a legal loophole to rebroadcast a foreign signal, as well as the fact that Ahmet Özal, the president's son, was one of its partners. This breach became a trickle, then a flood. Media ownership soon became a glittering prize with the ability to spin the day's events, giving proprietors political clout. There has been a great deal of joint ownership between print and broadcasting, and media personalities tend to straddle both fences.

This plethora of private media dramatically opened up the debate in Turkey. Live talk shows on the issue of the week started in the early evening and went on until dawn, an indication that in post-martial-law Turkey one could say pretty much whatever one liked and even for as long as one liked. New soap operas made people curious about other parts of the country and other lifestyles. Turks saw their recent history of military coups dramatized, and there have been series about mixed Greek-and-Turkish couples, Kurdish businesswomen, and ultranationalist mafia. Miniseries and popular entertainers became a vehicle of soft power, establishing Turkish influence in a wider region.

A new Radio and Television Supreme Council (RTÜK) was set up to regulate the broadcasting environment. In its early days the RTÜK became infamous for ordering stations to cease broadcasting for twenty-four or forty-eight hours, as punishments for infringements of its code. It still maintains a firm, if less overtly draconian, hold. There is, for example, a ban on people smoking, and in old films cigarettes are pixelated out. The courts have blocked access to Internet sites on grounds of public decency, restricted access to Google services for technical reasons (while it was trying to stop users from circumventing a legal ban on YouTube), and briefly deprived legions of Turkish bloggers access to their journals over a copyright dispute on Blogspot, which was being used by football fans to relay links to pay-for-view matches.

The government has been rightly accused of intervening in the press to limit criticism, and it is certainly true that the editorial independence of the TRT is circumscribed. The news it delivers is not so much one-sided in favor of the government as anodyne and cautious, so as not to give offense. No Turkish government suffers criticism gladly and it has been the covert policy of successive governments to control the flow of news. At the same time, governments are very sensitive to what is reported and respond to pressure—hence the perverse motive to intervene.

Organizations like the Committee to Protect Journalism or Journalists without Borders have drawn attention to attempts by government to tame opposition media with tax audits and attacks on press groups' nonmedia interests. Journalists writing about Kurdish issues still face legal harassment, although the days (in 1994) when the offices of a pro-Kurdish newspaper in Istanbul could be blown up and the perpetrators never caught are hopefully at an end. Successive governments have encouraged their friends to buy into the media and tried to punish media barons who oppose them by making commercial life difficult. Advertisers are scared off from placing ads with newspapers that are willing to publish and be damned. This has been the fate of *Taraf*, a badly financed but strong-willed paper that has broken stories embarrassing both to the government and to the military. Reporting restrictions on ongoing cases are onerous and appear designed to protect the judicial system from fair criticism.

The picture suggested by international NGOs with a brief to protect media freedom is that the Turkish state, armed with an antediluvian statute book, prevents the press from doing its job. Yet it is certainly the case that private media groups have been willing accomplices in their own capitulation. Self-censorship is a norm, and quite respected opinion columnists regularly have their pieces spiked out of the proprietor's fear of offending the powers-that-be. I offer my own experience of having worked on a Turkish-language newspaper and having been tried in 1999 on charges of having caused an institution of the state (in this case the military) to be held in disrepute—a charge which then carried a maximum six-year sentence. My conclusion at the end of this process was that the courts had tried me fairly under a bad law. The body I held accountable for my brief misfortune was my own newspaper, which failed to defend me in print and which later ceded to pressure to have both myself and other of its columnists dismissed.

The Turkish media has proven a poor watchdog over its own freedoms because of its unholy alliance with government. In too many cases, media ownership has been the "loss leader"—and purely a means to pursue non-press financial interests. A fitting sequel to my own story is that the newspaper proprietor was subsequently held in prison on remand charges of fraud after a bank he owned collapsed with nearly $1 billion of debt. The media group is now owned by a business group that supports the current government, the deal financed by state-owned banks.

What is the role of the military in Turkey?

The Turkish armed forces take a broad view of their mission to defend the realm, and have at times appeared to be less concerned with external threats than an enemy within—identified variously as political radicalism, forces of internal religious reaction, Kurdish separatism, and, on more than one occasion, the country's own elected government. So independently minded a military sets Turkey at odds with its NATO allies, let alone the European Union to which it aspires to join. However, a not-insignificant proportion of the Turkish population has accepted the military's relative autonomy as a counterbalance to the excesses of party politics.

While it is clear that the military is not immune from the corruption that infects Turkish politics, it is perceived by the public as behaving in a more disinterested way than other organs of the state.[2] This is largely because career officers do not cling to their appointments past their allotted span. The chief of staff serves for three years and then retires. Turkish politicians, traditionally, have to be dragged off their pedestal and even then manage to climb back on. All Turkish men have to serve in the army—fifteen months in the case of ordinary conscripts and twelve months (or six if they do not elect to serve as noncommissioned officers) for those with university degrees. It is a secular rite of passage, and friends are often dispatched[3] to do their military service in convoy with car horns blaring and ritualistic hoopla. The military is not an alien institution but one which every family in Turkey has personal knowledge.

It is a mild paradox that the military acquired its role as self-appointed guardian even as Turkey itself became more democratic. Atatürk very pointedly sent the military back to the barracks once the Republic had been declared and he himself hung up his uniform. Atatürk was succeeded by his prime minister, İsmet İnönü, who had himself been a heroic commander during the War of Independence. If the army was happily excluded from politics in the first decades of the Republic it was because there was no contradiction between its own esprit de corps and the philosophy of the one-party state. The inclusion into NATO of Turkey in 1951 did not so much provide a distraction for the nation's officer class as highlight their sense of deprivation as they began working with armies more modern than their own. By the late 1950s the Turkish economy was in tatters and those on a fixed income, including the military, bore the brunt. Resentment turned to anger at what they saw as the government's populist strategy and its betrayal of the secular revolution to court a religious rural vote. The 1960 coup was as much a junior officers' coup—although the support of a general (later president), Cemal Gürsel, was crucial to its success.

For some on the Turkish left, 1960 was an example of the "good coup"—one which restored the integrity of the Turkish state and which established the notion that the military could enter the political arena and then, unlike the generals of Latin America, withdraw once their work was done. This was not the view of the Turkish right, who were in power then and in the subsequent two coups. If the left still believed that only a coup could bring about radical change, they were cruelly disillusioned by subsequent military interventions that established order through wide-scale arrest and torture. During the 1980–1983 period of martial law, some fifty persons were hanged for treason, but more than three times that number died in prison and 14,000 people were stripped of their citizenship.

No martial law authority in Turkey has believed it could continue in power indefinitely. In practice, Turkish generals have proven themselves unconvincing politicians, and the armed forces have proved far more adept at taking power than controlling what happened after democracy had been restored. In 1983 the voters soundly rejected the party groomed by the military and chose instead the new Motherland Party of Turgut Özal, which was the group least tainted by military associations. The electorate even voted in a referendum in 1987 to lift the ban on pre-1980 politicians who were busy behind the scenes restarting their old parties under different names. The military may have been successful in driving an Islamicist party out of power in 1997, but this simply cleared away the "dead wood" of an older generation of politicians and opened a path for the breakaway AK Party to win the elections in 2002. In 2007, the military again tried to assume the role of principal opposition, covertly organizing mass rallies, and issuing stern warnings to the government not to elect as president someone they regarded as unwilling to uphold Turkey's commitment to secularism. The then chief of staff General Yaşar Büyükanıt warned on a 2007 visit to Washington that "never since the inception of the republic in 1923 have we faced such serious threats and risks." However, the economy was booming and even the military never had it so good. That same year, the military pension fund OYAK happily sold its bank to the Dutch giant ING for $2.7 billion. The government called an early election and won a landmark victory.

Could there be another military coup?

It seems improbable that the military will be in a position to remove, or even to aspire to unseat, an elected government in the foreseeable future. For a start, the military has always acted with a sense of its own legitimacy and with respect for their own chain of command. It is hard to imagine a scenario that would allow the armed forces to take charge of government while still retaining the approval of the country, maintaining discipline among their own rank and file, and winning the support of the international community and to do all this without upsetting the financial markets.

This is not to say that the military has abandoned all hope of retaining its independence from elected government or controlling the domestic agenda. However, once deprived of the "nuclear option" of a full-blooded coup, it becomes much easier for its political power to be whittled down. While not all postwar presidents have been members of the military, the armed forces once regarded that position as theirs by right. Even that is no longer the case. The AK Party government has tried to reduce its dependence on the military even for security and has announced plans to up the role of the police in combating Kurdish insurgency. Even so the government in its third term of office has taken to making a show of military force in foreign policy, not just against the PKK lodged in Northern Iraq but also against Syria, Israel, and Cyprus in the Eastern Aegean. There is clearly a tipping point beyond which it would be reluctant to demoralize its own military or deprive it of the very sabers they need to rattle.

In the past, economic and political chaos has been the cue for military intervention. Now a military coup would be the cause of instability, not its remedy. And yet there is evidence that some senior officers and their cheerleaders were prepared to ferment that very chaos in an attempt to reestablish their control. The exposure of that plot, or what the press calls the Ergenekon Conspiracy, has been in some minds the Armageddon between civilians and the military for control of state power.

What is the Ergenekon Conspiracy?

"Ergenekon" is the popular name given to a series of long-running legal investigations that began in 2007. The growing list of those accused—hundreds—includes lawyers, journalists, small-time Mafioso, and even university professors. The principal defendants however have been members of the military. At one stage there were 250 retired or serving officers in prison awaiting trial, including 30 (or one-tenth) of active generals and admirals.

"Ergenekon," the codename that the conspirators are alleged to have given their own network, refers to a mythical land of milk and honey where a Turkic tribe took refuge after being routed by the Tartars. They grew so fat and prosperous, the story has it, that they could not renegotiate the alpine pass, so that when it came time to reconquer their lands the only solution was to light a furnace in the heart of a mountain made of iron ore until it melted away. Today it refers to another sort of meltdown. The conspiracy's alleged modus operandi was to use the bomb and the bullet, as well as the planted newspaper headline, to create a climate of public opinion that would make it difficult for governments to carry out reforms. However, the ultimate aim was to create conditions ripe for a military coup. The Ergenekon prosecutor identified the torture and murder of three Christian missionaries in the city of Malatya in 2007 as part of a pattern of provocations with the evidence suggesting that the conspirators were planning or at least capable of even more heinous acts.

The conspiracy came to light with the seizure in 2007 of a cache of hand grenades in a house associated with a retired officer, weapons reported to match weaponry used in an attempt to bomb *Cumhuriyet*, a newspaper of the Kemalist Left—the implication being the attack was staged to make the country believe it was under threat from a radical Islamic movement. The discovery was connected to a series of other seized documents. In 2007, the now-defunct *Nokta* magazine published the diaries of a naval commander that outlined a strategy for provoking a coup three years earlier. The coup attempts had codenames like "Blond Girl," "Moonlight," "Sea Sparkle," and the far less romantic "Glove." The independently minded *Taraf* newspaper, which began publishing in 2007, became a source of highly sensitive leaks that included secret meetings between high court judges and senior commanders. It published other stories highly embarrassing to the military high command suggesting officers had failed to inform men on the ground of an imminent Kurdish guerrilla attack in order to ambush and embarrass the government's political initiative to expand Kurdish rights. *Taraf* also revealed the existence of a huge stash of documents allegedly to provide evidence of a coup attempt codenamed "Sledgehammer," devised in the immediate aftermath of the AK Party's initial victory in 2002. Among a long list of excesses, its plotters toyed with provoking the Greek air force to shoot down a Turkish plane and with bombing two prominent Istanbul mosques. These revelations led to another round of high-level arrests in July 2011 that, in turn, led to the protest resignations of the chief of staff and the commanders of the army, navy, and air force. The new chief of staff, Necdet Özel, is reputed to be someone who would be reluctant to involve the military in political intrigue.

Turkey being Turkey, there are those who accuse the Ergenekon prosecution itself of being a conspiracy, an attempt to intimidate the opponents of the government, deal a blow to the prestige of the army, and undermine secularism. The prosecution has fueled such accusations through the careless wording of an extremely long indictment and also in highly visible early-morning raids to bring in for questioning prominent suspects whose involvement in a vast conspiracy beggared credulity. Among them was the now-deceased head of a charity to promote women's education who was interrogated while in the middle of a course of chemotherapy. The prosecutor also ordered into detention in March 2011 two journalists who had not only supported the Ergenekon prosecution but had been critical of the prosecutors for not going far enough in enquiry into the murder of the Armenian editor Hrant Dink. Defense lawyers also maintained that anachronisms in documents leaked to *Taraf* indicated they were forgeries. Many of those charged have been refused bail and while in the past it was not uncommon for ideological foes of the regime—Kurdish or leftists—to serve long periods in remand while awaiting trial, it was not usual for pillars of the establishment let alone military officers to suffer such a fate.

The parallel trials, investigations, and arrests have taken so complex a trajectory that the details well exceed this book's rubric of "what everyone," or indeed what any sane person, needs to know. The case remains sub judice, and speculating on the verdict in proceedings that will go on possibly for years would be a mistake.

However, for the Turkish military to try to unseat its own government would not be without precedent. Certainly I and many of my journalistic colleagues long took for granted the existence of a dedicated office somewhere in the armed forces whose job was to plot how to remove the sitting government from power, much in the way that every army draws contingency plans to invade a potential foe. The officers in our hypothetical planning room probably did not even consider they were committing an offense. So to give names and dates to this supposition requires no great leap of faith. The military did try to rattle their swords at the government in a very public way in 2007 and tried to influence the outcome of the general election that year but without success. How far the coup plotters might have gone remains a matter of speculation, but it is widely accepted that Hilmi Özkök, chief of the general staff between 2002 and 2006, refused to support any coup attempt.

Yet if the Ergenekon trial is in the interests of democracy, it also serves the interests of a government that becomes stronger as the military retreats. The actual trial process has cowed opposition, and the wire-tapping of anyone peripherally involved in the enquiry, including journalists, has become routine. That the military is capable of a coup does not strain belief, it is also credible that the government is capable of influencing the prosecution to its own political advantage. One consequence of the Ergenekon trial, and of the AK Party's long tenure of power, is that the gap between state and government has narrowed considerably and it is much harder for elected politicians to avoid direct accountability.

What sort of Constitution does Turkey have?

Turkey has a history of constitutionalism that predates the founding of the Republic. One of the initial demands of the Young Turks in 1908 was the restoration of the 1876 Constitution abrogated by Sultan Abdülhamid II. In 1921, the rebel Nationalists adopted a simple constitution that was expanded into the founding articles of the state in 1924. In 1961 Turkey penned a new constitution while under martial law, and though it may seem counterintuitive the intention of that document was to broaden participation in the political process. It was written very much as a reaction to what was seen as the elected tyranny of the recently deposed government. The 1961 Constitution created a second chamber, guaranteed rights of organized labor, and allowed for state-owned universities to govern themselves autonomously. Turkey's current constitution, also promulgated under military rule, is anything but a charter for liberalism. It is very much a "yes, but ..." constitution in the sense that it allows for full rights and freedoms—except in circumstances where these rights might threaten the integrity of the state. That document and the attending legislation have been modified many times, such as when a raft of amendments was adopted through a national referendum in September 2010. One of those amendments lifts the immunity that the authors of the 1980 coup enjoyed from prosecution. In general, however, the spirit of the law is to protect the state from the citizen rather than the other way around.

The 1982 Constitution created a powerful state apparatus whose inner workings would remain in the control of the Constitution's authors or their political heirs. Governments might come and go, but as long as the Turkish president could appoint judges and key bureaucrats, and even heads of universities, and as long as the military was sworn to uphold the secular state, the basic principles of the Republic—as laid out in 1961—would remain immutable. An old guard accused those of pressing for change or a new constitution altogether of trying to found a "Second Republic."

This would explain the alarm which the Turkish establishment felt as they saw the state apparatus slip into the hands of those whom they regard as their ideological foes—the AK Party, whose Islamic leanings they held in deep suspicion. Understanding as they did the full power of the Constitution, they experienced that same sinking feeling Dr. Frankenstein did when he realized that the creature he created had been given the wrong brain.

This might explain, as well, the moral quandary in which a non-Kemalist government, like the AK Party, finds itself when the muscle and authority buried in the subclauses of the Constitution and accompanying legislation fell into its own hands. Does it use that power to consolidate its own rule and risk dividing society; or does it dismantle the 1982 Constitution, replacing it with a different sort of charter altogether? The AK Party fought the 2011 election with the promise to produce a new constitution that will command a wide-scale consensus. However, this is an exercise fraught with political hazard and could easily go astray. The fate of a new constitution will be an important index of where Turkey is headed.

The AK Party government is often accused of consolidating its own rule and becoming more authoritarian. Evidence includes the strong-arm tactics with which police often quell student demonstrations, or the pressure exerted on an opposition media, or the long period of detention which those accused of conspiracy to overthrow the government spend in jail while their case is still being heard. It also has been accused of fostering its own business elite, using armies of tax auditors to intimidate those who fail to support it. That these sorts of abuses are as old as the Republic may be an explanation but not an excuse.

A key sticking point is the office of the presidency. Turkey has a parliamentary and not a presidential system, and the prime minister has by far the most important job. But the president's role is not entirely symbolic. He (there have been no women up to now) is responsible for the final selection of high-level appointments in many branches of government—even, as we've seen, university rectors. The Turkish establishment, which includes the military, is anxious to see the post go to someone who shares its values and ideological certainties. This would explain the great unease with which the military viewed the election of the incumbent, Abdullah Gül.

Though by most definitions a political moderate (in 2010, the Queen of England, on behalf of the very sober British foreign policy think-tank Chatham House, awarded him the accolade of Statesman of the Year), he was schooled in Islamic-oriented politics and his wife wears a headscarf.

Gül was elected by a vote of parliament for a single term of seven years. That system has been changed. The president will be chosen by a popular vote for five years and can stand for a second term. This has led many to speculate whether Turkey is moving toward a more presidential system and, if so, whether Prime Minister Erdoğan is after the prize. There is the danger that the efforts to produce a new constitution may become bogged down in the question of redefining the role of an executive president.

6

SOCIETY AND RELIGION

What role does Islam play in Turkish public life?

Turkey is both a Muslim-majority country and an avowed secular state. Reconciling these two identities has proven surprisingly complicated. While Turkey lays claim to serving as a cultural ambassador between faiths in a post-9/11 world, its own domestic political agenda sometimes reflects the emotionally charged debate about the compatibility of Islam with democratic governance. There is a basic divide between those who believe Islam is being manipulated by political forces to derail the Western orientation of the Turkish state and those who counter that this Islamic peril is a specter raised by elements trying to cling to a very undemocratic influence and privilege.

Article 24 of the 1982 Constitution guarantees freedom of religion and conscience but with the proviso that these freedoms do not threaten the integrity and secular character of the state. At the same time, the Constitution implicitly recognizes faith as one of the bonds of citizenship by making religious and ethical instruction mandatory during primary and secondary education. Islam in Turkey remains influenced by the Hanafi School or what had been Ottoman orthodoxy—the oldest and arguably the most liberal of the four schools of Sunni jurisprudence. Schools teach this practice rather than comparative religion.

Turkish secularism, therefore, is not so much a separation of mosque and state as it is the state's right to assert its primacy over religion. The government still funds a huge religious establishment, the Presidency of Religious Affairs (DİB), which licenses after-school Koranic courses, administers Turkey's allotted pilgrimage quota for the Hadj, publishes books, and makes moral pronouncements. While it does not build or maintain mosques, it does provide stipends for the nation's clerics, who, in turn, are expected to preach a prepared message from the Friday pulpit.

The DİB is by its own admission a much-modified version of the Ottoman religious authority, the Sheikh-ul-Islam. Yet the Ottoman Empire was far from being a cleric-run theocracy. The clergy were regarded as functionaries rather than divinely inspired. A state bureaucracy worked to codify laws involving taxation, commerce, the military, agriculture, and minority affairs—matters beyond the purview of religious law. Religious or customary law has no status in Republican Turkey, having been replaced with a Swiss-inspired civil code. However, the DİB can still set itself the ambitious project to codify the *hadith*, the orally transmitted tradition of the Prophet's teachings, a project largely intended to confirm Islam's compatibility with democratic values and universal rights.

Osama bin Laden was among those who put his finger on the resulting anomalies. In one of his infamous post-9/11 video appearances, he explained that he was out to avenge "eight decades of pain, humiliation and shame." The reference, Turks grasped at once, was to the creation of their own Republic in 1923 and to the decision of Atatürk to plow salt into the notion of a religiously empowered state. The 1924 abolition of the Caliphate—the leader of the world Islamic community and a role enjoyed by the Ottoman sultan—was a renunciation of an authority that could transcend the border of the nation-state. Moves like the outlawing of the self-governing religious orders were intended to prevent religious institutions and what today would be called "networks" from challenging the new regime. The formal adoption of the Gregorian calendar, of Western-style timekeeping in place of "mosque time," and, indeed, the whole tenor of Republican reforms were all premised on the view of Islam as an impediment to Turkey's attempts to catch up with the West. They were attempts to deconsecrate, or secularize, the totems of religious life. In 1930, a short-lived uprising led by a cleric in the Western town of Menemen (during which the local military commander's head was cut off and paraded on a pole) was not a threat to the new regime so much as a challenge to its confidence that the population at large had signed onto its modernization project. The incident helped confirm in the Republican imagination that religion was counterrevolutionary and needed to be monitored and contained.

Even so, the anticlericalism of the nation's founders began to soften in the postwar multiparty era as Atatürk's top-down modernization was replaced with top-down democratization. In the 1950s there was greater tolerance for Islam—including the reopening of many mosques and schools of divinity—and the government allowed mosques to resume the practice of summoning the faithful to prayer in Arabic rather than in Turkish. Although the core Republic guard saw this as pandering to populist sentiment, later it was the military itself—during the 1980–1983 period of martial law—which viewed religion as a force of social cohesion and made religious instruction compulsory. The rationale for the coup had been the violent street warfare between gangs of left-wing and nationalist youths. Religious radicalism was regarded as something of a spent force, and the military hoped to co-opt Sunni Islam into propping up old-fashioned nationalism. The result was a worldview known as the "Turkish-Islamic synthesis."

The success of the overtly Islamicist Welfare Party in the 1994 local elections and in general elections the following year obliged the military to doubt the wisdom of their benign view of religion. This was the election that launched the career of Recep Tayyip Erdoğan, who was to prove the military's most able foe and who was able to maneuver his AK party into the political mainstream. The AK party repackaged its commitment to Islam as a question of private conscience and democratic choice.

Is Turkey in danger of becoming a fundamentalist state?

This question is one often posed by those who fear that Islam is the main obstacle to Turkey's fuller integration into the West or that it prevents the country from achieving its ambition of full democracy. I would argue that the more alienating force is a crude nationalism that in the past has served as a cover for government corruption and political and economic isolationism. Yet many nonetheless fear that Turkish society is becoming a Kulturkampf between rival secular and Islamic-oriented elites.

The most obvious antidote to polarization is the ability of a population to accommodate and thrive from diversity. Some women wear headscarves, some have piercings, and some have both. Around 65 percent of Turks are teetotalers; those who indulge can now choose from an increasing array of wines from boutique vineyards that have become the passion and playthings of a Western-oriented elite. The residents of the conservative Central Anatolian city of Kayseri joke about those who attend Friday prayers but leave for a weekend at the nearby tourist hotspots of Cappadocia, much in the way the burghers of Philadelphia once made for Atlantic City on a Saturday night to evade the ban on selling alcohol in the early hours of Sunday.

Turkey still regards itself as a home of the world's revealed religions and actively promotes "faith tourism," hoping to attract three million visitors to religious monuments and sites in 2012. The Archbishop of Constantinople, or the Ecumenical Patriarch, is the first among equals of the 300 million adherents of the Orthodox faith worldwide, and the title dates back to the sixth century. Bartholomew, the present incumbent, still celebrates liturgy in the Church of St. George by the shores of the Golden Horn. The castles and churches of the medieval Armenian kingdoms are scattered through eastern Turkey and the seat of the Armenian Patriarchate has, since 1461, been in Istanbul. The Roman city of Sardis near the Aegean contains the restored remains of a third to fourth century A.D. synagogue, and the Arhida Synagogue in Istanbul remains active more than 500 years after it was first built. Guidebook in hand, one can visit the basilicas of the Eastern churches, including Chaldean Catholic churches and Assyrian monasteries where the liturgical language is ancient Aramaic. Though still functioning, these monuments to Anatolia's multiconfessional past are at best vestigial. The communities they serve have barely survived a twentieth-century legacy of nationalist upheavals and subsequent exodus. Turkish-born non-Muslims now account for less than 1 percent of the current population.

There is a gap between the rhetoric of tolerance and the actual practice. Opinion surveys commonly report individuals' reluctance to live next to people of faiths different than their own. However, there are not that many non-Muslims to put this abstract prejudice to the test. One might expect, to take a nonreligious example, that there would be much greater tension between Kurdish and non-Kurdish communities, particularly during periods when the Kurdistan Workers Party (PKK) has been on a violent campaign. While it would be foolish to deny prejudice exists, dire prophesies of intercommunal tensions between Turk and Kurd simply have not materialized. Perhaps a common faith remains a unifying force. To inject a personal note, one of the most attractive features of living in Turkey as a foreigner is the quality of respect and civility that invests the exchanges of everyday life.

It would, therefore, be unwise to see discrimination against non-Muslims as a function of an increasing Islamization of Turkish society or of the ascendancy of the AK Party rather than as a part of the nationalist legacy already referred to. The Greek Orthodox community has also been the victim of tit-for-tat retaliation over the treatment of the Turkish communities in Eastern Greece or in Cyprus. If anything, religious minorities have benefited from the greater openness that the AK Party requests on behalf of its own mainstream constituents. The unease that Turkey feels about allowing full expression of other faiths stems in part from its own insecurities about Islam. An interesting case is the Orthodox seminary on Heybeli (Halki in Greek) Island off the coast of Istanbul, which served as a private and therefore illegal institution of higher education; it closed in 1971.

This is of great concern to the Patriarchate, which relies on the institution to train future clergy. Since then, the door has been opened to private universities albeit under the supervision of the Board of Higher Education—a solution that the Orthodox Church cannot accept. This has led to an impasse that, in turn, has become a diplomatic embarrassment. The fate of Halki is often on the agenda when Turkish statesmen travel abroad, and it has been the subject of resolutions from both houses of the U.S. Congress. The real problem is not that the government wants the school to remain shut but rather that, if it allowed priests to be trained in institutions outside its control, it would come under pressure to extend that same right to "unlicensed" courses in Islam.

Not all Islam in Turkey is mainstream. As pointed out above, there is a sizable Alevi community. Alevi is a form of Shi'ite Islam, but unlike in Iran, where Shi'ism has reinforced a theocratic orthodoxy, Alevis have been part of a culture of dissent in Turkey. Their faith incorporates elements of mysticism and folk religion and exhibits an indifference to many of the practices associated with mainstream Islam—including obligatory fasting during the month of Ramadan or even the pilgrimage to Mecca. Alevis are sometimes regarded as the front line in the defense of Turkish secularism inasmuch as they are treated with condescension or at best overlooked by the religious establishment. Many Alevis resent seeing their taxes going to support that establishment or a school system that teaches a variant of a faith very different from what they practice at home. Indeed, one could argue that they have long been the victim of the intolerance which Turkish secularists fear may one day rebound on themselves.

At the same time, it would be wrong to gloss over the mutual suspicion between those adopting a pious lifestyle and those who adhere to a more latitudinarian one. Both have reason to fear the other's intolerance. Commentators speak of the informal "neighborhood pressure" and of a conservative ascendancy forcing people to conform to mores they might not choose themselves. Turkish secularists wonder whether they will be made to wait on the wrong side of the barriers they themselves erected. Historically it is the pious who have been excluded from public life.

The answer to those who worry that the AK party is a fundamentalist party in liberal clothing is that it has been in office since 2002 and has had ample time to show its hand. There is evidence that it believes it has the mandate to legislate on issues of private morality and enforce more strictly those laws and ordinances that already exist. However, it seems unlikely that any Turkish government would make a sudden move that would excite opinion both at home and abroad. In 2004, Erdoğan did propose making adultery a felony, and he backtracked precisely when the ensuing uproar began to affect Turkey's attempt to get a seat at the EU negotiating table. In fact, adultery had been illegal in Turkey, but the law governing it was declared unconstitutional in 1996 because it applied a far stricter standard for women (mere infidelity) than for men (essentially, taking a mistress). The never-enacted law apparently was intended not to tame philandering modernists but to discipline pious men who thought themselves entitled to take on additional partners, sanctioned by Islamic law but not by civil code. Legislation came into effect in 2011 that has made it more difficult to serve alcohol at some types of events or for alcohol firms to sponsor sporting events. These restrictions, as well as higher taxes on alcohol, were justified on grounds of public health and not morality. The AK party government is equally anti-smoking.

However, its general disapproval of alcohol is seen by secularists as the not-so-thin edge of the wedge.

The pious may be against the consumption of alcohol, but they show no sign of being against consumption per se. Turkish sociologists talk about a newly empowered Islamic bourgeoisie. Islamic (i.e., "non-interest" or "participation") banking in 2010 accounted for a mere (and static) 4 percent of total banking assets, and there is scant public discussion concerning the morality of credit cards or bank interest. One reason to doubt there will be a sudden "majoritarian" imposition of an Islamic regime is that there is no groundswell of people who see a major incompatibility between the demands of their faith and the life that they are already living.

On the whole, it would be absurd to see mosques as providing an underground network of dissent. Some women do complain that their religious headscarf subjects them to discrimination. However, their principal demand—akin to that of the American civil rights movement—is to be accepted into the mainstream rather than to overthrow the existing order. Women who wear headscarves are often reluctant to see their own fight in the context of a larger battle for human rights—for example, the right to be educated in Kurdish—presumably because this would recast their demands in a far more radical light. Indeed one could make a convincing argument that religion, far from presenting a threat to the Republic, has proved to be a safety valve and a force of social integration during an intense period of urbanization.

This is reflected in the proliferation of mosques, though their construction is not state-funded. In 1990, well before commentators suspected Turkey of lurching to the religious right, 1,500 mosques were being built every year—at a far brisker rate than new schools.[1] For the most part these buildings are replicas of sixteenth-century classical architecture, with slender minarets and cascading domes. In this sense, they parallel the Gothic-style churches that were a feature of the post–Industrial Revolution neighborhoods of Victorian Britain, evoking the sacrament of history to celebrate not just God but the foundation of community. This has particular resonance in Turkey, where communities were often built in defiance of planning procedure and through the quasi-legal occupation of public land. Mosques were buildings that authorities would think twice about before tearing down.

It is not just the tenacity of religion that has taken secularists by surprise but its ability to adapt to modernity and itself become a vehicle of change. One of the most prominent faith movements was founded by the charismatic preacher Fetullah Gülen. The movement that bears his name has managed to prosper less through sermons in the mosque and more through the media, think tanks and NGOs, financial services, commercial enterprises, and even universities. The Gülen Movement has created a huge network of nonreligious private and charter schools in Turkey as well as in over 100 other countries.[2] These schools are far more emissaries of Turkish culture—a privately financed form of public diplomacy—than centers of Islam. In this they are the mirror image of elite foreign-language high schools (German, French, Italian, and English) in Turkey itself and have become vehicles for Turkish commercial penetration into parts of the world once beyond its reach. The schools provide a high standard of education, and they are particularly popular in the former Soviet Union because of their discipline and because the teachers do not drink. Proselytizing, where it exists, is very much an afterschool activity.

Gülen himself advocates an "alternative" modernity that involves a very explicit rejection of the proposition that Islam is incompatible with contemporary life. The Islam he teaches, though culturally conservative, has an emotional appeal as well as a quietist or mystic component that makes it different from a fundamentalist state religion. Gülen-associated institutions, for example, are active participants in interfaith dialogue.

The size of his following is difficult to estimate. Three million is a frequently cited figure, but a recent *Time* magazine article put the figure as high as six million. What seems beyond dispute is that the movement has huge influence. *Zaman*, the house newspaper of the movement, is among Turkey's largest circulating dailies and actively supports the AK party government. By contrast, it did not back its predecessor, the Welfare Party, which had a much narrower, anti-Western, and Muslim Brotherhood feel. Some see the Gülen Movement as the Islamic incarnation of Calvinism—a belief system that embodies the spirit of capitalism and that legitimates itself through the worldly success of its adherents. Others, far less charitably, believe that, if not Gülen himself, then those who shelter under his umbrella have tried to create beachheads, or "sleeper cells," within the bureaucracy and particularly within the police. That the "Master Teacher" (or "Hoca Efendi"), as Gülen is respectfully called, has spent more than a decade in self-imposed exile on an estate in Pennsylvania only makes him a more shadowy and sinister figure from this point of view. The suspicion is, as one Turkish minister once said to me, that he owes his allegiance not to where he grew up but, as the proverb would have it, "where he ate."

In the spirit of full disclosure, I have had an opinion column in *Zaman*'s English-language affiliate. I often disagreed with the editorial line of the paper, which, like all Turkish newspapers, is reflected in the way it reports the news. It very clearly circles the wagons when it feels the Gülen Movement itself is under attack. However, no one prevented me from making my own views or disagreements known. This happy state continued until I argued that the government's fight against antidemocratic forces was taking a decidedly undemocratic turn—proof of which was the detention of two journalists accused of being part of an Ergenekon conspiracy to overthrow the state. One of those arrested, Ahmet Şık, wrote an unpublished book bitterly critical of the Gülen Movement, which the authorities attempted to ban but failed when the unedited manuscript began circulating on the Internet. My simple point was that as a newspaper we had an obligation to defend Şık's freedom of expression in order to protect our own integrity. The article was never published in my paper and cost me my job.[3]

Who are the Kurds?

If Turks were the last of the Ottoman ethnicities to get their own nation-state, the Kurds arrived at history's party too late. There are anywhere between 28 and 35 million Kurds, inhabiting a region that straddles Turkey, Iran, Iraq, and Syria, with smaller populations elsewhere, including Armenia, Azerbaijan, and Lebanon. This geographic diversity suggests that Kurdish identity is shaped by a variety of competing forces and that ethnic solidarity with fellow Kurds across borders is often overshadowed by the concerns and politics of the countries in which Kurds actually find themselves. In Turkey, Kurds form a majority in fifteen provinces in the southeast and east of the country, with the metropolitan city of Diyarbakir being the unofficial capital of the Kurdish region. There is also a large diaspora both in Western Europe and in coastal Turkish cities like Adana and Izmir. Istanbul, on the diametrically opposite side of the country from Diyarbakir, is almost certainly the largest Kurdish city in the world, in the way that New York City is home to the largest number of Jews.

Defining what constitutes Kurdish identity is no less problematic than defining race and ethnicity in other parts of the world in which there have been centuries of migration and shifting political boundaries. The official Turkish census does not poll ethnicity. The *CIA Fact Book* estimates that Kurds make up 18 percent of Turkey's population, but if one defines a Kurd as someone who actively identifies himself as Kurdish, or who either speaks or is exposed to a Kurdish language, then surveys based on sampling suggest that figure is probably nearer to 12.5 percent, or close to 10 million people.

Kurdish is not a single language but an Indo-European linguistic group that shares many similarities with Farsi or Persian. The two main Kurdish parties in the north of Iraq, for example, draw from two distinct linguistic communities. The Kurdistan Democratic Party has as its constituents Kurmanji speakers, whereas the Patriotic Union of Kurdistan in the southeast, along the Iranian frontier, is supported largely by those speaking Sohrani dialects. Turkish Kurds are also mainly speakers of Kurmanji but there are also Zaza speakers—although (to further complicate matters) not all Zaza speakers identify themselves as Kurds. That dialects are not always mutually comprehensible is often used to disparage the idea that there could ever be a common Kurdish identity. However, Turkish nationalists who make this argument do so with the hindsight of nearly nine decades of intense nation-building that included huge institutional support for a standardized Turkish. Kurdish, by contrast, has never been a medium of public discourse in Turkey or of education— despite the fact that some children begin school without knowing Turkish.

In 1991 I went to visit a group of Kurdish nationalist MPs in a Diyarbakir hospital. They had been beaten by riot police after attending the funeral of Vedat Aydın, a local politician almost certainly murdered by the security forces. Together in the ward, they spoke Turkish among themselves. Today's Kurdish nationalists are far more militant about using their own language.

There are small numbers of Christian, even Jewish, Kurds as well as those of Armenian ancestry who have been assimilated as Kurds. However, the overwhelming majority are Muslims and are historically devout. Many of the great leaders of Kurdish social movements, including those in the early twentieth century, have been sheikhs (religious authorities). Many Zaza are not Sunni Muslim but Alevite.

Kurdish society is traditionally rural, subdivided into tribal affiliations that have historical origins in the parceling and defense of pastureland. Kurdish tribes under the Ottomans enjoyed semiautonomy and existed as a buffer among the Safavids of Iran. Central government was adept at co-opting tribal leaders, or *ağa*s, into the political process. In the late nineteenth century, sons of *ağa*s were sent to elite schools in Istanbul. In more recent times, *ağa*s sit as MPs.

It is fair to say that much of the rest of Turkey looks at Kurdish society through a glass darkly and sees tribal organization as imposing primitive loyalties and archaic kinship relations. More useful would be to think of tribes as a form of pre-representation or alliances that negotiate with the political mainstream. Likewise, radical Kurdish politics draws from inequalities within Kurdish society and not simply on the denial of Kurdish identity.

Where do Kurds fit into Turkish society?

For all its claims to be a melting pot of civilizations and a mosaic of different cultures, Turkey has been continuously blindsided by the problem of accommodating its own ethnic diversity. A principal reason lies in the foundation of the Turkish Republic and the perceived need to impose a new national identity on a war-stricken nation. Kurds posed an obvious challenge, first because they formed a distinct and regionally concentrated linguistic group that was not Turkish but also because they were overwhelmingly Muslim and therefore not an "anomalous minority," as defined by the Treaty of Lausanne.

Though Kurds were readily recruited to fight the War of Independence, commanders of Kurdish irregulars felt betrayed by the very secular, highly centralized, and very Turkish character of the new state. There was a major uprising in 1925, which drew from resentment against the abolition of the Caliphate as much as it did from a nascent Kurdish nationalism. That rebellion became reason and pretext to reinforce the authoritarian character of the regime in the rest of Turkey. A loyal (and certainly not Kurdish) opposition party, which counted among its number heroes of the Independence, was abolished; newspapers in Istanbul were shut down; and tribunals were established to eliminate not just Kurdish dissent but opposition in general. From the beginning of the Republic, the Kurdish issue, and specifically fear of Kurdish secession, has become inextricably linked to the problems of Turkish democratization and of the reliance on forms of repression to keep society under control.

Turkish officialdom has historically pursued a policy of assimilation, using both carrot and stick. It might appear as a caricature to liken Kurdishness to homosexuality in the American military ("don't ask, don't tell"), but it is the case that as long as one doesn't insist on a Kurdish identity, Turkish society does not discriminate. Kemal Kılıçdaroğlu, who became leader of Turkey's main opposition party in 2010, is (probably) an Alevi Kurd from Tunceli, that is, a minority within a minority, but his election produced no Obama-like catharsis of a nation coming to terms with its past. The stick is reserved for those who assert a Kurdish identity, and Turkey is only now relaxing legislation that denied any semblance of Kurdish cultural rights. It is something of an urban myth that Kurds could only be referred to as "Mountain Turks." It is not Kurdishness per se the courts have prosecuted. Rather, they have pursued incitement to separatism or aiding and abetting terrorism. Yet, merely writing or even singing in Kurdish has been taken as proof of this intent. Leyla Zana, an MP elected in 1991, was stripped of her office and served ten years in jail. Her conviction for membership in an armed gang was disputed by Amnesty International, which accepted her as a prisoner of conscience. Her real crime was presumed to be the rider she added in Kurdish when swearing her parliamentary oath of allegiance.

Turgut Özal, president at the time of the First Gulf War, is credited with realizing that the Turkish establishment had to change its attitude toward its own population if it were to play a role beyond the country's southeast border. He was responsible in 1991 for repealing an infamous 1983 law, which in effect made it illegal even to speak Kurdish on the street. He died in 1993 before he was able to undertake more radical reforms. However, even his more cautious political rival, Süleyman Demirel, spoke of Turkey's "Kurdish reality" as prime minister in 1991, even if he did not act on that perception. In 2005 Prime Minister Erdoğan made a "winds of change" speech in Diyarbakir, promising "more democracy, more civil rights and more prosperity." Later his government promised a "Kurdish Overture" to come to terms once and for all with Turkey's Kurdish problem. However, it became frightened by its own bravery when in 2009 a group of Kurdish rebels returned in battle fatigues across the Iraqi border under an amnesty program, arriving not as repentants but to a tumultuous (and cleverly stage-managed) hero's welcome. The "Kurdish" part was subsequently diluted into a catch-all "Democratic Overture," and progress to formulate a specific program of reform began to stall. One tangible result, however, is that as of 2009 there is now a Kurdish-language state television station, although it steers clear of controversial subjects, and Kurdish philology and language courses are being offered in a few Turkish universities. At the very least, Turkey has managed to decriminalize those who take pride or interest in being Kurdish.

What lies at the heart of Turkey's Kurdish problem?

Even to ask this question gets on some Turkish nerves. A still widely held view is that the Kurdish problem is simply one of terrorism, or of troublemakers trying to scratch an itch where none exists. The issue, thus defined, centers on the guerrilla campaign conducted by the Kurdistan Workers Party (better known under its Kurdish acronym, PKK) and its now-imprisoned leader Abdullah Öcalan.

The PKK was one of many underground revolutionary movements born in the 1970s, but it is unique in that it managed to broaden its support by giving voice to a proscribed Kurdish nationalism. It has since taken on many different names and incarnations; the party has military and political wings and the air of a popular movement. In 1984 the PKK first took up arms against not just the military but also "state" targets like schoolteachers and fellow Kurds who cooperated with the authorities. Turkish security forces, along with teams of counterguerrilla fighters, met force with heavy-handed force. They sought to deny the PKK room to maneuver by evacuating and burning villages suspected of providing militants with logistic support. At the same time, the authorities created a "village guard" system of a pro-government rural militia in an attempt to divide and rule the countryside. Many villagers felt themselves caught between the authorities and the PKK as if between a rock and a hard place. If the heavy hand of the authorities acted as the PKK's recruiting sergeant, the grief of slain Turkish soldiers' families is often paraded, by contrast, as an argument against making any concessions or even acceding cultural rights. The conflict is estimated to have cost over 40,000 lives, including civilians, PKK members, and Turkish soldiers.

The British journalist Robert Fisk, no sympathizer with Turkey, once likened Öcalan to a murderous psychopath in the ruthless tradition of the Palestinian Abu Nidal.[4] Kurdish nationalism, nurtured in the hothouse of émigré politics, does at times appear to be a distorted reflection of the Turkish nationalism it opposes. The PKK victims have also included rivals and dissidents within their own ranks. However, so long as the state restricts channels for identity politics (a Kurdish nationalist party that served as the political wing of the PKK was closed down by the courts as recently as 2010), the PKK retains its legitimacy in many eyes.

In effect, the PKK was the product of a vicious process of natural selection after all other channels of dissent were eliminated. This is not to say that were Turkish politics to become as unproblematic as Norway's, support for the PKK would vanish. The group has championed the cause too long. However, it does mean that the PKK would be forced to accommodate dissent.

After real panic in the early 1990s that they were losing the fight with the PKK, the Turkish security forces became far more adept at using counterguerrilla tactics, taking the fight to the mountains, and reducing the level of conflict. In 1998 Ankara, fortified by a close understanding with Israel, put pressure on Syria to expel Abdullah Öcalan (nicknamed "Apo") from his safe house in Damascus—which paradoxically cleared the way for a reconciliation with Syria and, arguably, a deterioration of relations with Israel. The PKK leader was subsequently located in the Greek embassy in Kenya by an FBI team investigating the bombing of the U.S. embassy in Nairobi. He was abducted and taken back to Turkey to stand trial.

With Apo behind bars and cooperating with his captors and the PKK in disarray, Ankara had the chance to do what it said it would never do under duress and address demands for cultural rights. And though it was a window of opportunity the then coalition government failed fully to exploit, preferring to believe that victory had been won, there was some progress. This was also a period when Turkey was trying to push forward an application for EU candidacy and to do so it had to confront its record on human rights. In 2002 the ultranationalist National Action Party, as junior partners in that government, acquiesced in a vote to abolish the death penalty, in effect telling their supporters that Öcalan would never hang.

At the same time, the events of 9/11 in America had created some sympathy for Turkey's own longstanding fight with terrorism. The harsh measures adopted by Western states to fight al-Qaeda appeared to confirm a long-cherished Turkish maxim—that national security required the sacrifice of liberties. The PKK found themselves in a difficult position. They themselves adopted a carrot-and-stick strategy, punctuating ceasefires with acts of violence, using the threat of instability to kick-start a political process in which they would play a lead. This tactic became more difficult to sustain in a world where "no negotiating with terrorism" became the rhetorical norm. Some European nations which had tolerated PKK political offices, partly to ensure a quiet life for themselves, ceded to pressure to declare the group a terrorist organization. Ankara still continues to complain about the level of cooperation the PKK receives, with Denmark coming for particular censure as being home to a Kurdish broadcasting channel that Turkey says is the voice of Kurdish radicalism. However, in 2011 a recording leaked on the Internet provided evidence that Turkey's own National Intelligence Organization (known by its acronym MİT) had itself been in secret negotiations with the PKK for at least a year, moderated by Norwegian officials.

Those who deny the existence of a Kurdish problem point out that the southeast of Turkey is not purely Kurdish. Roads once punctuated by military checkpoints are now safe to travel. Many Turks or Turks of Arab descent have deep roots in the region and there are communities of Assyrian Christians. The years of conflict have taken their toll, and there are now new and desperately poor neighborhoods of those forced to migrate from the countryside. Old Diyarbakir families complain, as do their Istanbul or Izmir counterparts, that their home no longer resembles the cosmopolitan city of their youth when there was a mix of ethnicities and religions. At the same time there are new middle-class housing estates, populated by people perhaps not always happy to call themselves Turks but happy to play the role of Turkish consumers. There are also doctors and teachers and other civil servants assigned from the rest of the country on a rotating compulsory service.

On the whole, however, even those without sympathy for the PKK accept that the people of the southeast of Turkey have a legitimate grievance even if there is a divergence of views on what underlies the Kurdish problem.

A problem of underdevelopment: Particularly those to the left of center in Turkish politics tend to define the issue as one of poverty, income differential, and regional disparity. There are the occasional bombings in regions outside the southeast; that there has been no sustained urban guerrilla campaign in cities like Istanbul, Izmir, and Adana, all of which have large Kurdish populations, is cited as evidence of an inverse relation between political demands and standards of living. The counterargument is that police and intelligence are simply more effective in large cities, including those of the southeast.

The Kurdish regions are considerably poorer than other parts of the country and social indices—the number of girls who complete primary school, or rates of infant mortality—are among the worst in the country. (The exception is Istanbul, where poverty and social problems are "imported" by new migrants to the city.) Successive governments hint that this is not the result of a lack of public spending but of cultural resistance to development.

The problem of course is not just how much is spent but where it is spent. Huge sums are allocated to hydroelectric projects or to the military counterinsurgency. At the same time a fund used to subsidize families who keep their children at school, and which actually succeeds in getting girls to get a primary-school diploma—a key factor in encouraging them to join the workforce—is trivial by comparison.

A geopolitical problem: Turkish concern about its own territorial integrity translates into a concern that its neighbors not set a dangerous example by allowing political autonomy for their own Kurdish population. There was a time when Syria, Iran, Iraq, and Turkey engaged in a "Mexican standoff"—actively encouraging Kurdish rebels on the other side of the border to use as leverage against anyone trying to do the same to them. This was no longer possible when Iraqi Kurds gained de facto autonomy after the 2003 Second Gulf War.

Ankara's worst fears were realized in the aftermath of the First Gulf War in 1991 during which the U.S.-led coalition forced Iraqi troops out of Kuwait. Washington appeared to encourage the Iraqi Kurds to rise up against Baghdad, and then betrayed the subsequent rebellion by allowing Saddam Hussein to remain in power. As the helicopter gunships of the Republican Guards turned on Kurdish fighters, hundreds of thousands of Iraqi Kurds fled toward the Iranian and Turkish frontiers, creating a vast humanitarian crisis. Turkey, under the glare of international publicity, tried to stop the influx of refugees by erecting camps in the no man's land along its mountainous border, all of which helped focus international attention on Ankara's treatment of its own Kurds. Turkey then found itself having to offer Iraqi Kurds safe haven until those refugees could go home. That safe haven inevitably became the foundation of today's Kurdish Regional Government (KRG) in Northern Iraq as well as a refuge for the PKK, which then stepped up their armed campaign against Turkey itself. The Kandil Mountains in Northern Iraq near the Iranian border continue to harbor PKK fighters.

This explains Turkish reluctance to allow U.S. troops to use Turkish territory to invade Iraq for a second time in 2003. Today Ankara remains committed to preserving the integrity of Iraq but must come to terms with the virtually independent and potentially oil-rich KRG. Turks ask themselves why the United States, so determined to fight terrorism, should have tolerated the existence of PKK bases in the mountainous regions of the Iraqi border near Iran. The practical answer is that the KRG's own political constituency will not allow it to turn against Turkish Kurds and that the American occupying forces in Iraq had more than enough to cope with without stirring up yet another hornet's nest. Such answers do not stanch the widely held belief in Turkey that Western powers use Kurdish insurrection to keep Turkey weak. Some suspect the United States arms a sister organization of the PKK to foment Kurdish resistance in Iran. These views persist despite an agreement under which the Pentagon makes real-time intelligence available to the Turkish military in order to track PKK fighters infiltrating over the Iraq border. Washington has also committed itself to providing Turkish forces with drones and other anti-insurgency hardware.

Turkish politicians often portray PKK attacks not as part of some intractable domestic problem but as "contracted" by outside powers. At the same time they are only too aware that the Kurdish issue affects Turkish ambitions to play the role of a stabilizing power in the region. "Peace at home, peace in the world" was Atatürk's much-quoted mission statement of Turkish foreign policy. That has been paraphrased as a commitment to "zero problems with neighbors" by Ahmet Davutoğlu—a foreign minister appointed in 2009 but the long-standing architect of the AK Party's external policy. That vision will flounder if Turkey cannot come to terms with a problem in its own backyard.

A problem of corruption, incompetence or conspiracy—and, of course, democracy: While Turkey may accuse the outside world of exploiting the Kurdish conflict for devious ends, many in Turkey are now troubled by the suspicion that there are those within the country who have long done the same. The argument goes that if the PKK did not exist, the Turkish military would be forced to invent them—and may have on occasion done just that. Tansu Ciller, who had little interest in the Kurdish issue when she became prime minister, became an instant hawk when, the very day her cabinet was formed, the PKK reportedly shot and burned their way through a remote village, killing twenty-eight people. More recently, *Taraf* began reporting incidents where commanders ignored, either deliberately or through incompetence, satellite intelligence of PKK attacks. In one notorious case from February 2008, a post at Aktütun, located near the border with Iraq and Iran, was overrun and seventeen soldiers died even though there was ample satellite photographic warning.[5] Some acts of provocation are not in dispute. In 2005 an angry crowd apprehended three undercover military agents who had set off a bomb in a bookstore in the town of Şemdinli along the Iraqi border. The public prosecutor who tried to pursue the case up the ranks of the chief of staff was dismissed and only six years later were the suspects re-arrested to be put on trial.

Such incidents take place in addition to the "dirty war" fought in the 1990s when Kurdish intellectuals, journalists, and politicians were the targets of extrajudicial execution. The units inside the security forces responsible scarcely bothered to cover their tracks.

The prima facie case is that an expensive conflict (one estimate is $300 billion to date), and one being fought in terrain that serves as a staging post for much of Europe's heroin, was bound to create its own momentum. The very clear implication of the Susurluk scandal mentioned above—the car accident suggesting a connection between organized crime and security forces—was that state-sanctioned assassins were being used to fight the PKK in exchange for a free hand in the drug trade from Afghanistan and Iran to Europe.

In 1983, after Turkey went back to civilian rule, thirteen of the provinces in the Kurdish regions remained under a form of emergency law with the last two only regaining normal status in 2002. In 2010 a sufficient number of AK backbench MPs defied their own leaders to defeat a constitutional amendment that would have enhanced legal protections for political parties. Although the amendment would have rescued their own party from a threat posed by an aggressively secular Constitutional Court, the rebel MPs thought it important to sacrifice their own interests if it meant extending legal protection to Kurdish nationalists. Kurdish nationalist MPs also voted against an amendment which they judged provided them no protection at all since it still allowed for parliamentary consent for prosecutions to shut down a party. They calculated that this would protect the AKP but not themselves. that afforded them no protections at all.

In 1989 Eastern and Central Europe rejected Soviet-style totalitarianism and embraced a democratic ideal. Yet Turkey, which might have been expected to reap a dividend from the end of the Cold War, became more authoritarian. It became embroiled in a costly fight to suppress Kurdish insurrection and has in some measure has been corrupted by it.

Is there a Kurdish solution?

Another way of asking this question is: What do Kurds in Turkey want? Full cultural rights? A process of truth and reconciliation? Devolution, or simply the prospect of prosperity? Hardened Turkish nationalists believe that any concession to Kurdish identity will lead to political secession. Having defined the fight with the PKK for so long as a struggle against separatism, they take for granted that separatism must be the enemy.

On the other hand, not even the PKK Party openly calls for an independent state and at various stages has declared its only ambition is to democratize Turkish society. Many would accuse the PKK leadership of simply trying to cling to the brute power afforded them as the head of a paramilitary organization. Many Kurds may, in their hearts, hope for a Greater Kurdistan. However, they fear that a political entity sited in the "Bermuda triangle" of Iraq, Iran, and Syria would find it hard to stay afloat. Indeed, greater autonomy is opposed by some in the Kurdish heartland itself. Diyarbakir may be a nationalist stronghold, with a party close to the PKK getting 65 percent of the vote at the 2009 mayoral election there. That still leaves another 32 percent who voted for the AK Party. Certainly, the PKK wants to be part of a settlement and to see Abdullah Öcalan emerge from his prison cell. This is hard for Turkish mainstream politics to concede. It is hard enough for any national political party to consent to Kurdish primary education, let alone a major devolution of power or some sort of federation.

There are competing forces at work. Many are fed up with the violence and have no desire to return to the grim old days of attack and retaliation. At the same time, a new generation refuses to kowtow to Turkish nationalist orthodoxy. Kurdish activists are themselves divided. Abdullah Öcalan's ability to hold his movement together from a prison cell via his lawyers is limited. There is always a more militant faction prepared to embarrass those in favor of a settlement based on compromise. The government's ability to divide and rule, however, is limited and depends on its willingness to make major constitutional concessions to Kurdish identity.

The current government has tried to defuse Kurdish demands by promising a share in the good life. Before the Gulf War, Iraq was Turkey's largest trading partner, and better relations with Syria and Iran mean the region's natural markets were opening up at last. The AK Party's Islamic sympathies implies there is a "higher" identity that could unite Turk and Kurd. To some, that identity is defined not by God but by the European Union. "Turkey's road to Brussels goes through Diyarbakir," former Prime Minister Mesut Yilmaz once said, the implication being that Turkey would not be ready for membership until the Kurdish southeast was ready too. But the reverse is also possible—that Kurds will feel happier to be part of a Turkey that shares its sovereignty with Europe. However, the reality of EU membership remains a long way off.

The liberal consensus is that Turkey must at last draw a line in the sand. On one side is lawful dissent and the demand for cultural and minority rights, and on the other is the use or threat of violence. The only solution to the Kurdish problem lies with the Kurds themselves. It is certain that Kurds will become more vocal and more sophisticated about challenging the Turkish nationalist component of the state and also more insistent about demanding fuller political and cultural rights. The question is whether it is too late for such a solution to emerge. There is every probability that Turkey will do what it has done these past decades and muddle through.

What is the status of women in Turkey?

When Turkish women read of laws and practices in Muslim-majority nations that discriminate against their sex or punish their sexuality, they think kindly of the founding vision of the Turkish Republic. Every schoolgirl knows that Atatürk freed Turkish women from the veil and polygamous marriage and replaced Koranic law and traditional custom with the European civil code. Men in white tie and women in backless frocks danced arm-in-arm across the floor in the Republic Day balls during the 1920s, a theatrical demonstration of women's new access to public and professional life. Women were given the franchise in 1930 and voted in municipal elections that year. However, as late as 2005 police used batons to disperse an unauthorized International Women's Day demonstration in Istanbul. And while this latter incident may not be typical, it suggests why feminists are not as grateful to their male liberators as the official history would have them feel. Women realize that they may have been lured into declaring victory in a battle which has only just begun.

Indeed, a 2010 World Economic Forum study on the gender gap put Turkey well at the bottom of the international league of equality (126 out of 134, below Egypt and Iran and just above Saudi Arabia; the United States was in 19th place and the United Kingdom 15th, while Iceland leads the list). Turkey's poor performance on key issues of equality of representation in the workforce, in health, and in education is all the more remarkable for being so totally at odds with its public's own perception.[6]

The presence of women in politics is often regarded as a key index of overall social attitudes. In 1993 the aforementioned Tansu Ciller, an economics professor, became Turkey's first woman prime minister and did so without belonging to a political dynasty. She failed, however, to be a trailblazer for women's rights (nor, her many critics would argue, to be an advertisement for women in politics). Of the 27 ministers (in 2010), two portfolios—education and women and family affairs—were held by women. In 2002 there were 24 women in the Turkish parliament (4.2 percent), a figure that rose to 50 (9.2 percent) in 2007—assisted by the disproportionately large number of women sponsored by the Kurdish nationalist party who were elected as independents. That figure rose again in 2011 to 14.3 percent or 79 deputies. In Britain, women made up 3.5 percent of MPs in 1983, rising to 9.2 percent in 1992 and 22 percent in 2010. In the United States, women comprise 16.8 percent of Congress in 2011, more than triple the percentage in 1991. The upward trend in Turkey is in part due to the campaigning efforts of KADER, an NGO that aims at boosting women's presence in politics. Their billboards depict prominent women wearing moustaches (asking if this is what it would take to get women elected) and shame the main parties just a little.

Many use a narrow definition of liberation to argue that Turkish women enjoy a Western lifestyle. From that perspective, a lunchtime journey through the shops and restaurants of the central business districts of many Turkish cities presents a picture little different from that of Paris or New York.

There are, by contrast, districts and parts of the country where women are far less visible or where they feel the need to negotiate public spaces modestly attired. This does not, of course, mean that the former "modern" sector is liberated and the others not. Some of the most voluble critics of patriarchal attitudes are conservative women who know all too well the concrete ceilings in the workplace and public life. Many see the problem rooted not so much in Islam as in patriarchal attitudes that diehard secularists have also failed to tackle. Hence the adage: "Atatürk liberated Turkish women but forgot to tell the men."

When I asked a friend, a prominent professor of social science, her greatest complaint as a Turkish woman, she replied it was when men treat her as a nonperson—the taxi driver who does not talk to her directly but through the third party of a male companion. She described the failure of Islamic feminists as similar to that of politicians: unable to conceive of women outside the context of a family unit. So while family planning is long established in Turkey (a law dates from 1964), the husband is required to give his consent in the case of abortion. Protecting the right of children to know the identity of their father is the rationale behind the 2010 ban on women receiving eggs or donations of sperm from fertility clinics abroad. Prime Minister Erdoğan attracted much notoriety for urging families to have at least three children in order to maintain a workforce able to support an aging population. (It is not advice that has been heeded; the average family sizes are not that different from the United States—2.18, as compared to 2.06.) This may be because Turkey makes few provisions for working mothers. Infant mortality statistics are also high—although this is in part the result of regionally skewed income distribution.

Many Turkish women, however, confront not only male attitudes but physical threats. Rates of domestic violence are disturbingly high. Some 42 percent of women over the age of fifteen have experienced physical or sexual violence at the hands of a husband or partner at some point in their lives, according to a 2009 study. That same study reports 18 percent of "women who have ever been married have at one point sustained serious injury in the same manner."[7] Well-publicized, determinedly vicious assaults by husbands against their wives have shocked the Turkish public into acknowledging the problem. The Ministry of Justice reported a jump in the annual murder rate of women from 66 to 953 in 2009. Yet the conclusion of a Human Rights Watch report was that the authorities were not simply underprepared but still unwilling even to recognize the problem. "Gaps in the law and implementation failures by police, prosecutors, judges, and other officials make the protection system unpredictable at best, and at times downright dangerous," it wrote.[8]

For all that, some of the most dramatic postwar reforms were carried out by the AK Party—as part of the preconditions for European Union accession talks. These included a reform of the penal code that went much of the distance in meeting demands of women activists. The changes were described by one campaigning NGO as succeeding in

safeguarding women's rights, and bodily and sexual autonomy.... All legal references to vague patriarchal constructs such as chastity, morality, shame, public customs, or decency have been eliminated and definitions of such crimes against women brought in line with global human rights norms. ... The new code ... brings progressive definitions and higher sentences for sexual crimes; criminalizes marital rape;

brings measures to prevent sentence reductions granted to perpetrators of honor killings; eliminates previously existing discrimination against non-virgin and unmarried women; criminalizes sexual harassment at the workplace and considers sexual assaults by security forces to be aggravated offences.[9]

Overall, the tide of legislation is far more powerful than the undertow of social attitudes.

Why are headscarves such a sensitive issue?

The headscarf issue has become Turkey's equivalent of the U.S. debate over gun control, where one person's freedom is another's tyranny. There are no real debates in Turkey about a woman's right to choose abortion (available on demand at up to ten weeks) nor about the morality of stem cell research. But the headscarf has become a defining issue. Many believe it is a right and obligation for pious women to cover their heads. Others see this as a deliberate affront and a symptom of creeping fundamentalism.

Women in Turkey dress as they please. However, state employees in schools, hospitals, and many echelons of the civil service are not allowed to keep their heads covered at work. The highest-profile test of this was the case of Merve Kavakçı İslam, a newly elected MP in 1999, who wore a headscarf and was not just prevented from taking her oath of office but actually stripped of her citizenship on technical grounds (not declaring her dual U.S. nationality). Most controversially, female students cannot wear a headscarf (although some universities bend the rules out of liberal principles if not common sense). The government and the head of the Board of Education are determined to see the ban lifted and it seems inevitable that it will soon become unenforceable. The Turkish military and many opposition politicians will boycott functions where head-scarved women are present; this precludes them attending functions hosted by President Abdullah Gül, whose wife covers her head.

Half of Turkish women tie a kerchief over their head when they go out in public. Secular Turks see this as "traditional" and not threatening. Few women (about 1 percent) cover their faces entirely or wear a black burka. It is the 11 to 15 percent of women who wear a "religious" covering who cause all the fuss. This consists of a scarf pinned around a cloth bonnet that covers the hairline above the forehead and often droops to the shoulders, covering the nape. Some women wear this with considerable panache, and use the word *türban* rather than the Arabic *hijab* to describe the results. This has its etymology (according to the dictionary of the Turkish Language Association) from the French word for a style of millinery made popular by the designer Paul Poiret around World War I. A 2006 survey, confirmed by follow-up research in 2009, revealed that while many *thought* the practice of wearing a turban was on the rise, the numbers were actually falling.[10] The study also revealed that some 70 percent of Turks didn't see the point of making life difficult for head-scarved women, though, paradoxically, it also revealed that attitudes on both sides were hardening.

For the pious, the issue has become the frontline of women's fight for a greater part in public life; secularists see it as a politically motivated assault on hard-won female emancipation. For some women, adopting the headscarf is a form of empowerment, allowing them to move freely in public space. Others feel threatened by young, educated, or upwardly mobile women deliberately adopting a symbol that pointedly rejects Republican values. This ambivalence was on display on the front page of the nationalist newspaper *Hürriyet*, which in May 2007 featured a photo of a student from one of Turkey's top universities, hips thrust forward, riffing away on a bright-red electric guitar at a rock concert while wearing a white headscarf. One of Turkey's ablest video artists, Kutluğ Ataman, has a piece entitled *Women Who Wear Wigs*, which consists of a series of competing monologues by four women with their heads covered—one is recovering from chemotherapy; one is a balding transvestite; the third is a leftist on the run and in disguise; and the fourth woman, whose face is never seen, wears a wig instead of a headscarf so that she can attend university. The work is in part a warning about recklessly attributing motives and categories.

In 2004 the European Court of Human Rights to which Turkey is a signatory declared in a landmark ruling that Leyla Şahin, a medical student at Istanbul University, had no inalienable right to wear a headscarf. Likewise, Turkey's own Constitutional Court disallowed a 2007 constitutional amendment that would have opened the way for covered women to attend university. Indeed, the government's intention to lift the ban was one of grounds for the public prosecutor's successful prosecution of the AK Party in 2008 for engaging in antisecular activities. The court shied away, however, from imposing the full penalty of ordering the democratically elected party of government to be shut down.

Whatever the juridical discussion, the popular debate over the headscarf seems to revolve over whether women cover themselves of their own free will or from community pressure—and whether that pressure, if unchecked, will not one day acquire the force of law. It is hard to see this happening, given that there is more than a critical mass of women who have no desire to wear a headscarf and who are supported by men. At the moment, it is the women who wear the headscarf who bear the brunt of discrimination. At the same time, there is the suspicion that men are quite happy to send women onto the frontline of Turkey's cultural war, and that were it a male sartorial habit to cause so much fuss, the matter would be quickly resolved.

What status do lesbian, gay, bisexual, and transgender (LGBT) people enjoy in Turkey?

Homosexuality is legal in Turkey. However, if women are still battling to be valued as individuals independently of the family unit, people whose sexuality might appear to threaten that family are under even greater pressure. Not only does the LGBT community not have a political champion, a former minister responsible for women and the family described homosexuality as "a treatable biological disorder,"[11] although she was replaced after the 2011 election by a woman of far more liberal opinions. There is no same-sex marriage or legal union in Turkey, nor is there a public debate on the subject. The Turkish armed forces defines homosexuality as a "psychosexual" illness that renders its sufferers unfit for what is otherwise compulsory military service. Conscripts once had to provide photographic proof to win exemption, although there was never any official requirement to this effect and the practice appears to have been dropped.

At the same time, the principle of antidiscrimination is enshrined in the 1982 Constitution. A legal case to shut down the Istanbul branch of the activist organization Lambda failed (the high court ruled "no clause exists in our laws that prohibits lesbian, gay, bisexual, transvestite and transsexual persons from assembly to form an association with aims of solidarity"), although equally telling is that the organization and similar institutions were prosecuted in the first place. Even then, acquittal was conditional on the association not encouraging behavior "with the aim of spreading such sexual orientations," a stance criticized in the European Union's 2009 annual progress report on Turkey. The EU Commission also cited the legal harassment of LGBT people through the misapplication of laws against public exhibitionism or offending public morality. The report further criticized the courts for applying the principle of unjust provocation to mitigate crimes against transsexuals and transvestites. The Turkish press has variously reported the dismissal of a football referee and a teacher of divinity when their homosexuality became public knowledge.

However, being openly homosexual in Turkey is much more a question of brooking social convention than defying legal statute. Istanbul has a lively gay scene, and the coastal resort town of Bodrum figures in European newspaper travel supplements as an ideal honeymoon destination for same-sex newlyweds. The conservative central Anatolian city of Kayseri has become a center for Iranian émigrés escaping the political crackdown following the disputed 2009 election, and among the exiles are men and women fleeing the potential death penalty for same-sex intercourse.

One could argue that modern Turkey's unquestionably puritanical stance toward homosexuality sits uneasily with traditions inherited from an imperial past. It wasn't until 1973 that the American Psychiatric Association removed homosexuality from its list of mental disorders, whereas there was a highly sophisticated Ottoman literary tradition of courtly male love in the sixteenth century.[12] Partly this is because a popular distinction is made between "active" and "passive" homosexuality, the latter being "real" homosexuals and the object of discrimination. Traditional Turkish society remains to some degree homosocial, that is, segregated according to gender, and it was this division that the Republic set out to abolish. Polygamous marriage, even in Ottoman times, was very much the exception, though arguably monogamous heterosexuality was one of the unpublicized Republican reforms alongside the better-advertised changes to the civil code. Placing the nuclear family onto a pedestal was central to the Nationalist and "modernist" project from the late Ottoman era.[13] It is a policy that the current government cherishes, and parliamentarians in committee rail against the declining rate of marriage and the increase in divorce.

There is a tolerance in Turkish society for the famous few—artists, designers, and entertainers who do not act as models for the rest of society. The best-known public figure was the widely adored singer Zeki Müren (1931–1996), regarded as one of the most able exponents of popularized Turkish classical music. But even he, like the American pianist Liberace—whose taste in clothes and accoutrements he appeared to share—did not openly admit to being gay. The case of another singer, Bülent Ersoy, is worth mentioning in brief. His struggle with his sexuality gripped Turkish newspaper readers at the time the country was entering a period of martial law in 1980, and journalists followed him to London when he underwent a sex-change operation. The martial law authorities banned Ms. Ersoy from the stage, and her successful appeal to have her sex change made legal and to resume her career seemed at the time dramatic evidence of Turkey's return to democracy after free and fair elections. She sparked the interest of the public prosecutor again in 2008 when she ridiculed a fellow judge on a Turkish *Pop Idol*–style contest for "speaking in clichés" when praising the martyrdom of Turkish soldiers killed in the Kurdish conflict. She would be reluctant, she said, to send a son of hers to die in a war that was the result of other people's intrigues.

Why doesn't Turkey concede there was an Armenian genocide in 1915?

In the dying years of the Ottoman Empire, the wartime government in Istanbul sought to contain Armenian rebellion in Eastern Turkey. It did so by forcibly deporting large sections of the population toward what today would be the Syrian border. That this resulted in hundreds of thousands of casualties and the elimination of communities with centuries-deep historical roots is not in question. It is how to characterize this destruction that has become the subject of bitter and at times unseemly controversy.

To Armenians worldwide, genocide is fact, not historical disputation. A commemoration occurs every April 24, referring to the day in 1915 when some 250 prominent Armenians were rounded up in Istanbul—an incident seen as part of a larger plan to eradicate the Armenian presence in Anatolia. Turkish historians themselves paint an unflattering picture of the Young Turk government that led the Ottoman Empire into World War I. Modern political scientists trace Turkey's postwar history of coups, and of a state insulated from democratic supervision, to the secretive committee that frustrated constitutional rule after seizing power in 1913. On the surface it might seem strange that Turkey would stake so much of its own credibility defending a predecessor empire whose immediate legacy it had itself disowned. Yet it has become part of the catechism of today's Republic that what happened in 1915 was part of the exigencies of war and not premeditated.

An official Turkish view—promulgated by the Turkish Historical Association and embraced by the population at large—is that Turks were themselves the initial victims of ethnic cleansing. Armenian revolutionaries, operating behind the czarist advance in 1914 through the Caucasus and far into Ottoman territory, mopped up a Turkish population now caught on the wrong side of enemy lines. It was this initial betrayal which, when the fortunes of war turned, prompted the expulsion of an Armenian "fifth column" and which lay at the heart of the Armenian tragedy. That various Armenian communities, such as in Izmir and Aleppo, were spared deportation is cited as evidence that there was no master plan for a "Final Solution." Cholera and famine (as well as attacks by Kurdish irregulars) also took their toll on the files of refugees. If blame is to be apportioned, the argument runs, it falls on Armenian revolutionaries who disturbed centuries of coexistence between Muslims Muslims and Armenians. These radicals consciously followed the proven strategy of the successful nationalist uprisings in the Balkans—tactics arguably adopted later by the PKK—which was to stage provocations that would prompt government retaliation, rally an alienated population to their side, and in the end win Great Power sympathy and intervention in their cause.

This version of events was in part a response to a campaign by the Armenian Secret Army for the Liberation of Armenia (ASALA) that assassinated forty-one Turkish diplomats between 1975 and 1984. The ASALA's demands went beyond genocide recognition and called for the return to Armenia of its western territory (that is, Eastern Turkey). The deaths of their colleagues alerted the Turkish Foreign Office to the need to fend off the 3 R's: genocide *recognition*, leading to demands for financial *recompense*, and eventually territorial *restitution*. Some jurists would argue that no such linkage is possible and that recognition of genocide would not in itself pave the way to legal action since the (1948) UN Convention on the Prevention and Punishment of the Crime of Genocide (though recognizing that genocides have occurred "in all periods of history") is not retrospective.[14] This has not stopped Turkish officialdom's conviction that an acceptance of genocide would throw open a Pandora's box of unintended legal consequences. There are third-party cases—against Western insurance companies, for example, or the American leasing of formerly Armenian-owned land for defense bases—which may be affected by historical interpretation of events.

Many Turks are themselves the descendants of those forced into exile from the Balkans and Caucasus during a series of wars from the mid-nineteenth century up to World War I. They harbor their own bitter family memories and sense of resentment. Many ask why the world refuses to remember the far larger number of Muslim civilians who died at Russian hands in the northeast of Turkey and in the Caucasus after 1914.

Nonetheless, Turkey faces an uphill struggle to convince an academic community, let alone world opinion, that the many wrongs suffered by Muslim Turks made a right. Some genocide historians see 1915 as the dry run for the fate of the Jews under the Nazis; others say that what happened falls well short of that terrible standard, that the massacres were not premeditated and that local administrators and commanders played an important role in either encouraging or, in some cases, preventing violence. In that sense, the events were, they argue, far closer to the ethnic cleansing or intercommunal violence in the former Yugoslavia of the 1990s. The UN Convention, regardless, supports a far broader definition of genocide than "systematic annihilation." It refers to "acts committed with intent to destroy, in whole or in part, a national, ethnical, racial, or religious group." For example, the International Criminal Tribunal for the Former Yugoslavia in 2004 ruled that the deaths of some 8,000 Bosnian Muslim men in Srebrenica at the hands of Bosnian Serbs was an act of genocide.[15] Even Prime Minister Erdoğan described Beijing's 2009 brutal suppression of demonstrations by the Uighurs (Turkic) Chinese in Xinjiang province as "tantamount to genocide."

The number of those who perished in 1915 is the subject of dispute. Some demographers say the commonly cited figure of over 1.5 million deaths exceeds the number of Armenians then living in Anatolia. Yet even half that figure points to a tragedy of unfathomable proportions. An estimated 300,000 Armenians survived the war, but that community has to a large extent migrated elsewhere. There are currently between 60,000 and 70,000 Armenians still living in Turkey, mostly in and around Istanbul (a figure not dissimilar to the number of Armenian nationals estimated to be working illegally in Turkey).

It is not an offense per se to refer to what happened as "genocide" in Turkey but there have been prosecutions against those who do so under legislation (Article 301 of the penal code), which makes it an offense to insult Turkishness—as we've seen. The widely adopted convention is to refer to genocide as "the so-called genocide." The state broadcasting regulatory authority punished private television stations that broadcast a frank discussion of the issue in 2010. For long years, Turkish schoolbooks did not so much teach the official view as ignore 1915 altogether. It was not until 2003 that a minister of education in Turkey announced a school essay contest on the subject, and even those attending Armenian high schools complain of being taught of their people's betrayal of their country. In 2008 schools were provided with DVDs of a documentary commissioned by the armed forces with the title of an Armenian song "The Blond Bride." A case to have the distribution stopped on the grounds that the violent imagery in the film would promote enmity failed, but educational authorities recanted to some extent and said the film was intended to train teachers, not to be shown to pupils.

Ultimately, most Turks do not believe they are behaving hypocritically in denying genocide. In Germany, for example, the "culture of contrition" for what happened in World War II was nurtured when the country was under occupation. Disowning the Nazi past was a necessary act of repentance for admittance to the postwar congress of Europe. Something similar happened in 1919, when Istanbul was under Allied occupation. A tribunal was set up, and in what could well be described as the first modern war crimes trial, cabinet ministers and party functionaries were made to account for crimes that included the "deportation and massacre of Armenians." The Young Turk triumvirate was sentenced to death in absentia, along with four others.

However, the trial was transferred to Malta out of concern that the prison would be stormed by an irate populace and the proceedings eventually lapsed.[16] The new Republic allowed the matter to drop. It had achieved its own stasis in 1923 by casting off occupation and defeating rival nationalist forces, of which the Armenians were one. It would have been remarkable indeed at a time when Hitler and Stalin were consolidating power that Turkey would have engaged in a detailed process of introspection over what the previous regime had done to the Armenian population. It would have been all the more remarkable given that many of those who were to gain prominence in the new regime were co-opted from the old.

And yet attitudes in Turkey are changing. In 2005 three prestigious Istanbul universities challenged taboos by organizing a conference on the Armenian issue. The conference succeeded despite legal challenges, street protests, and the public discouragement of some ministers (and the private encouragement of other very senior members of the government). The assassination in 2007 of the Armenian newspaper editor Hrant Dink led to soul-searching in Turkey, particularly when evidence began to emerge that the killer—a member of an ultranationalist band—may have been deliberately incited to commit the murder as part of a larger conspiracy to sow unrest. A memoir (translated into English as "My Grandmother") by Fetiye Çetin, which involves the discovery that her grandmother was an Armenian orphan brought up in a Turkish officer's family, attracted much attention when it was published in 2008 and raised awareness that there were many others who had been forcibly assimilated. In 2011, the Turkish government apologized not for the fate of Ottoman Armenians but the massacre of Kurds in Dersim (modern Tunceli province) in 1937–38. While this was in part a ploy to embarrass the CHP opposition whose leader is from Tunceli and which was in power at the time, the breaking of so great a taboo led to inevitable speculation that that an apology to Turkish Armenians might be next.

There is also a renewed interest in the substantial cultural contribution Armenia made to the Ottoman Empire, be it through architectural exhibitions, cookbooks, or concerts—all of which are tactful ways of removing the public barriers erected by Turkish nationalism. Historians dealing with 1915 focus on a special forces unit that existed within the Young Turks who organized the deportations. As Turks uncover present-day cabals and conspiracies, it becomes increasingly credible that similar organizations existed within the state in 1915.

Turkish governments propose the issue should be resolved by an official historical commission (rather than by foreign legislatures voting at the behest of well-funded lobbies) and have long opened the archives of the period. Those archives have certainly been vetted, though they are sufficiently vast to escape simple weeding. For example, the most important source of records, the Prime Ministerial Archives in Istanbul, provides unflattering evidence of a policy of forced conversion of Armenians in the 1890s.[17]

Wasn't there another tragedy in 1915?

Perhaps another clue to Turkish attitudes is the other momentous event in 1915, when Allied troops launched an assault at Gallipoli to capture the Dardanelles. That battle, and the part played in it by Mustafa Kemal as a young commander, is celebrated as the birth of proto-nationalism in Turkey. A vast war memorial consisting of four massive columns topped by a concrete slab dominates the skyline and is visible to the ships that pass through those Straits. It is as if the architects took literally the instruction to design a cornerstone of the Turkish state. The memorial is very different in character from the carefully tended Commonwealth War Grave

Commission cemeteries nearby, with individual gravestones often marking the actual spots where soldiers from Britain and its then-colonies died. Britain projected power by its ability to preserve the memory of the individual soldier in the furthest corner of the globe. The Turkish style of monument celebrates the anonymity of sacrifice. Indeed, the monument was only completed in 1960, generations removed from the events it commemorated. It commemorates the defense of territory.

In Australia and New Zealand, the Gallipoli graves are also symbolic of the birth of the nation, but in this case through a loss of innocence. This in part explains why not April 24 but rather April 25 is observed each year as Anzac Day, without bitterness. Antipodeans blame themselves or the British, not the Turks. In the respective national histories, the encounter is now seen as something of a fair fight. Turkey assists in the Anzac Day commemorations willingly, and government officials often wonder out loud why the Armenians can't be more like the Antipodeans.

The answer, of course, is that Armenians were not an invading army but subjects of the Ottoman Empire.[18] The result is that there are no monuments in the east of Turkey, where facing the future meant developing collective amnesia over the trauma and shame. "Lest we forget" is the refrain to the Ode of Remembrance cited on April 25, when the Commonwealth remembers its dead. Turkey's attitude often seems to be that oblivion, even about one's own suffering, is the safer course.

What are the implications of genocide resolutions?

Turkey devotes considerable resources and political capital to trying to defeat measures in foreign legislatures that would either recognize the events of 1915 as genocide or would criminalize genocide-denial. At regular intervals, Turkish lobbyists square off against their Armenian counterparts in the United States, trying to prevent a nonbinding resolution commemorating genocide from reaching the floor of the House of Representatives, and it is this contest that attracts the most public attention in Turkey. As the centennial of 1915 approaches, and more and more legislatures take up the issue, Ankara finds itself increasingly isolated, forced to take niggling measures (the recalling of ambassadors, the canceling of government contracts, and a general posture of uncooperativeness) against countries which by rights should be its friends.

In the case of the United States, such retaliation might take the form of the withdrawal of strategic cooperation in some key area, such as U.S. access to the important İncirlik airbase on the Mediterranean, which is used to provision troops in Afghanistan and Iraq. American defense contractors are fearful that Ankara would cancel lucrative deals and are among those most vociferous in opposing such a declaration. Successive presidential administrations oppose the resolution, less out of support for the Turkish view of history and more because they do not feel it is the place of lawmakers to decide historical controversies, particularly if this means giving an offense to an important ally. Those in favor argue that survivors and their offspring have a right to have their government take a stand regardless of the international repercussions. Even so, the debate over the genocide resolution has become less about evaluating competing truth claims than a political arm-wrestle between competing Washington factions: an Armenian lobby that contributes heavily to campaign funds and a "strategic" lobby eager not to offend Turkey.

Until now Turkey may not have won the argument, but it has won the fight. Genocide resolutions have gotten past committee but never onto the House floor. Every April 24, like some apocalyptic Groundhog Day, Turkey holds its breath to see if the U.S. president will utter the "G" word in his annual address. It happened once, by Ronald Reagan in 1981, a year when Turkey was under martial law. Barack Obama pledged himself while a candidate to recognize the genocide but in his first year of office sidestepped this commitment by referring to the *medzyeghern*, the Armenian expression for the "great calamity." At least twenty nations, including Canada, Argentina, Russia, Lebanon, and France, have adopted some form of genocide resolution, and there is only so far Turkey can retaliate before it damages its own interests. It is probably this capacity for self-harm that concerns Turkey's allies most—that the perception of the world being lined up against it would simply lead to a retrenchment inside Turkey and a hardening of attitudes that would make internal discussion more difficult.

This explains, too, why even outspoken members of the Armenian community in Turkey are reluctant to push for genocide recognition. The same is true of even liberal-minded Turks, who believe that the price Turkey pays for ignoring its past has been to encourage the Turkish state's own sense of impunity. Many see genocide declarations by states as being less about establishing truths than as a form of Armenian Diaspora identity politics—a legal triumphalism that stifles dialogue between Turk and Armenian. In an interview I had with Hrant Dink before he was assassinated he described such resolutions as a pact between those who wanted to isolate Turkey and Turks who basked in that isolation. "I do not need another government to tell me what happened to my ancestors," he said, accusing Armenians of being fixated with their own tragedy and Turks by their need to deny it. "The only remedy is to help each other," he said.

Lately Turkey has tried to reopen its border with the Republic of Armenia itself, a border that it closed in 1993 to protest Armenia's occupation of the disputed Nagornoh Karabakh region in its war with Azerbaijan. In 2008 the Turkish president attended a World Cup Football qualifying match in Yerevan between the two national sides; the Armenian president repaid the compliment by attending a match in the Turkish city of Bursa a year later. This led to a protocol (still to be ratified) between the two countries in October 2009 intending to restore full relations. The logic of the agreement was that Armenia would pry open a frontier vital to its economy, and Turkey would be able to persuade those in favor of genocide resolutions that now was not the time to rock the boat. As of this writing, this deal has yet to happen, largely because of the leverage still held by Azerbaijan over Turkish foreign policy. Azerbaijan wants Ankara to keep the pressure on Armenia and uses the lure of cheap and ready energy to secure its cooperation.

7

CONCLUSION

What sort of future does Turkey face?

Since this is the last question, I allow myself the luxury of answering it obliquely, or at the very least with an anecdote or two. In 2007 I returned to Turkey after an absence of a year. Almost immediately on my return I was obliged to cover the story of the assassination of the respected Armenian journalist, Hrant Dink, whose death continues to haunt his friends. I regarded Hrant as a true patriot who had been put on trial both in the courts and in Turkish public opinion for views falsely attributed to him. The youth who pulled the trigger was soon caught and turned out to be a member of an ultranationalist band who may well have been manipulated into doing a deed whose implications he imperfectly understood.

However, in the immediate aftermath of the shooting I stood in front of a CNN camera in the street in which Hrant's *Argos* newspaper had its office. I became apprehensive as I saw a crowd gathering behind me. The newspaper is only a few blocks from the criminal court where in previous months I had seen Hrant confront jeering demonstrators at his own trial, and my first shocked reaction was that this, too, was a shameful assembly of bully-boy rightists come to gloat at his death. It was only slowly that I realized how very wrong I was, and that these were people who came to pay their respects to a man who had touched their lives. By the time I finished my work, the trickle of faces had grown into a sea.

Later, in Hrant's funeral cortege, 100,000 people and possibly more marched with "Spartacus-like" signs that they, too, were Armenian and they, too, were Hrant. If the person or people who wanted him dead had been hoping to provoke division, bitterness, and unrest, they must have been shocked to find that what they had stirred was unity, humanity, and hope itself.

It often takes people by surprise that Turkey still looks upon itself as a young republic. Afterall, it is on the verge of celebrating its ninetieth anniversary, which makes it younger than Great Britain but far older that the German Federal Republic. It has endured traumatic periods of martial law, but these have been less sustained than the long periods of dictatorships suffered by Spain, Portugal, and even Greece. Turkey was a one-party state until 1950; this is nothing compared to the majority of the new EU accession states, which until just over two decades ago were part of the Soviet System. However, Turkey's sense of being young is not mere vanity in at least three distinct ways.

The first is that its population is on average less aged than "old" Europe—which is the source of both dynamism but also popular expectation. The second is a recognition that Turkey is still catching up institutionally with "more mature" democracies. And the final sense, in mild contradiction with the second, is the belief that world history is spinning in Turkey's direction and away from older, tired civilizations. Literature from the end of World War I not only depicts Turkey as a collapsed empire but sees it as a doomsday vault for the values of a Europe in flames. Just as Constantinople was the "New Rome" in the fourth century A.D., the Turkish Republic was meant to be the new West. That rhetoric has never entirely gone away. There is often a dramatic mismatch between European sentiment, which may condescend to accept Turkey into its union, and a Turkey that believes Europe needs it to survive.

The truth is that Turkey has lost its youthful blush. It is at the very least adolescent. And, like an adolescent, it bristles to be taken seriously. It complains when it is not understood. It criticizes those it once regarded as its elders and betters for having made such a mess of the world. And while it pays lip-service to the counsel of others, it believes that it knows best. At the same time, it has the irritating tendency to blame others when things go wrong. It reserves the right to be fractious and rebellious, but at the same time it seeks approval and wants to be patted on the back. And of course everyone knows how thin-skinned, even annoying an adolescent can be—which explains the ribbing Turkey sometimes receives in the international press.

Whatever the truth of this description, it is certain that Turkey is coming of age and has both the appetite and the ability to play a greater role on the world stage. This will earn it greater respect but means it must grow accustomed to the critical scrutiny with which it once regarded others. All such efforts at leadership will be doomed if it does not increase the level and sophistication of public debate through more liberal education and a freer and more critical press.

A final story. The first newspaper article I ever wrote was about punk rockers in Northern Ireland. They had none of the painted Mohican hair-dos or pins in their cheeks and indeed no accoutrements more outlandish than blue jeans and short hair. When I asked them why they seemed so normal, the reply was, "In Belfast it doesn't take a lot to be different." Shortly after that I went to research a Ph.D. in Istanbul. The year was 1980 and the city and country were under martial rule. If everything seemed a bit grim, it was because there was not enough electricity being generated to make the street-lamps glow nor enough foreign currency even to import the beans to make Turkish coffee. It was a society in which if you looked different you would be stopped and asked to show your papers.

Although my hypothesis that acceptance of nonconformity and countercultures was a symptom of democracy might have been simplistic, I remember thinking to myself that one day young people would dye their hair orange and would feel free. And while it is true that there are people on the street with dyed hair, they are not so many. On the other hand, there are those who wear headscarves and those who don't, and the nation is overcoming inhibitions over its diversity and no longer attempts to conceal its differences. I do not believe all the orthodoxies of today will remain the certainties of tomorrow. Istanbul, the city I live in, is in so many ways annoying, particularly in its neglect of its unique natural beauty and its hurried disregard for its past. But one can no longer accuse it of being grim; it glows.

NOTES

Chapter 1

1. The correct answer is İsmet İnönü (1938–1950), Cemal Gürsel (1960–1966), and Turgut Özal (1989–1993).

Chapter 2

1. Caroline Finkel, *Osman's Dream: The Story of the Ottoman Empire 1600–1923* (London: John Murray, 2005), 3–4.
2. Seljuk Esenbel, "A Comparison of Türkish and Japanese Attitudes Toward Modern National Identity," in Günter Distelrath and Peter Kleinen, eds., *Fundamentalismus versus Wissenschaft? Zur identität des Orients in östlichen und westlichen Diskursen* (Bonn: Bier'sche Verlagsanstalt, 2002).
3. With another 10% permanently emigrating according to the American demographer Justin McCarthy, a prominent skeptic on the issue of the Armenian genocide. Yet even he puts the figure of Greek and Armenian deaths at 900,000 and calculates 3 million Muslim fatalities. *The Ottoman Turks* (New York: Longman, 1997), 387.
4. The main exception would be the province of Hatay on the Syrian border, which passed from French control to independence and finally to Turkey in 1939.

Chapter 3

1. *Türkstat*, 2006. Turkish Statistical Institute. www.turkstat.gov.tr.
2. *Betam Research Brief 09/39*, Bahçeşehir University, Istanbul 2009.
3. A problem highlighted by World Economic Forum data which put Turkey in 61st position in its 2010–2011 Global Competitiveness

Report: Turkey benefits from its large market, which is character-ized by intense local competition (15th place) and sophisticated business practices (52nd). The country also benefits from reasonably developed infrastructure (56th), particularly roads and air trans-port infrastructure, although ports and the electricity supply require upgrading. In order to further enhance its competitiveness, Turkey must focus on improving its human resources base through better primary education and better healthcare (72nd), addressing the inef-ficiencies in the labor market (127th), and reinforcing the efficiency and transparency of public institutions (90th).

4. UK Trade & Investment, *Sector Report: Agriculture/Turkey*, Ankara 2008.

Chapter 4

1. Hakan Yilmaz, "In Search of a Turkish Middle Class: Economic Occupa-tions, Political Orientations, Social Life-Styles, Moral Values." Research project supported by a grant from the Open Society Institute.
2. A study for the Open Society reprinted as Ali Çarkoğlu and Ersin Kalaycioğlu, *The Rising Tide of Conservatism in Turkey* (New York: Palgrave Macmillan, May 2009).
3. Karl Vick, "In Many Turks' Eyes, U.S. Remains the Enemy," *Wash-ington Post*, April 10, 2005.
4. Barack Obama, press conference, Ankara, 6 April 2009. See www. cnn.com/2009/POLITICS/04/06obama.turkey/index.html.
5. See Sinan Ülgen, "A Place in the Sun or Fifteen Minutes of Fame? Understanding Turkey's New Foreign Policy," *Carnegie Papers* (November 2010).
6. Quoted in Malik Mufti, "From Swamp to Backyard: The Middle East in Turkish Foreign Policy," in *The Middle East Enters the Twenty-First Century*, ed. Robert O. Freedman (Gainesville: University Press of Florida, 2002), 83–84.
7. "Timeline of Turkish-Israeli Relations, 1949–2006," produced by Brock Dahl and Danielle Slutzky for the Turkish Research Program of the Washington Institute for Near East Policy.
8. According to Yigal Schliefer, "A Setback for Turkey as Mideast Broker," *Christian Science Monitor*, February 6, 2008.
9. "Report of the International Fact-Finding Mission to Investigate Violations of International Law, including International Human-itarian and Human Rights Law, Resulting from the Israeli Attacks on the Flotilla of Ships Carrying Humanitarian Assistance." A/ HRC/15/21, September 27, 2010, paragraph 263, 53. See also Hugh Pope, "Turkey, the Flotilla and Israel: UN Report Deserves Calm Reading," International Crisis Group blog, http://www.crisisgroup. org/en/regions/europe/turkey-cyprus/Pope-Cyprus-The-UN-s-first-Mavi-Marmara-report-deserves-calm-reading.aspx
10. *Today's Zaman*, November 9, 2009.

11. "Report of the Secretary-General's Panel of Inquiry on the May 31, 2010 Flotilla Incident, September 2011," known as the "Palmer Report" after its New Zealand chairman.
12. Olga Keltosova, *Report on Domestic Violence*, Council of Europe, Strasbourg, September 2002, quoted in Ignacio Ramonet, "Violence Begins at Home," *Le Monde Diplomatique*, July 1, 2004.

Chapter 5

1. Freedom House stated this in its 2007 "Freedom in the World Report." The 2011 edition of that same report awards Turkey a could-try-harder three points (partly free), with seven being the worst score. *The Authoritarian Challenge to Democracy, Selected Data from Freedom House's Annual Survey of Political Rights*, 16. http://freedomhouse. org/images/File/fiw/FIW_2011_Booklet.pdf
2. The military was still the most highly regarded Turkish institution, according to a Pew Global Attitude Project of September 2010. At 72% this marked a decline from previous years (85% in 2007) but all institutions, from the prime ministry to parliament, displayed a similar fall in trust. Some 61% of those surveyed thought religious leaders had a good influence in 2007, which fell to 41% in 2010. http:// pewresearch.org/pubs/1720/poll-turkey-referendum-constitution-confidence-institutions-erdogan-negative-rating-nations.3
3. There is a complicated system of partial exemptions for Turks working abroad and the government, controversially, is introducing a system of exemption in return for a hefty fee.

Chapter 6

1. *Sabah*, April 11, 1990.
2. According to the literature produced by the movement. See http:// www.fethullah-gulen.org/op-ed/gulen-schools.html.
3. It was published in rival papers both in Turkish and in English (http://archive.hurriyetdailynews.com/n.php?n=a-dilemma-2011-04-07). The paper's editor justified the dismissal in his own column (http://www.todayszaman.com/columnist-240737-why-was-andrew-finkel-fired.html)
4. "Psychopathic Killer Who Is Great Hope of a Nation," *The Independent*, February 17, 1999.
5. Reported in *Taraf*, October 18, 2008. An interview with an editor of *Taraf* about these incidents in English (reprinted from the *Süddeutsche Zeitung*) appears at http://www.esiweb.org/rumeliobserver/2008/10/17/taraf-the-military-and-taking-sides/
6. Nigar Göksel, "Women in Turkey—What Is on Paper, What Is in Practice?" German Marshall Fund, August 31, 2009. Also, Ali Çarkoğlu,

"Public Attitudes towards the Türban Ban in Turkey," *Utrecht Law Review* 6, no. 2 (June 2010).

7. Turkish Republic Prime Ministry Directorate General on the Status of Women, Hacettepe University Institute of Population Studies, ICON-Institute Public Sector GmbH, and BNB Consulting, "National Research on Domestic Violence against Women in Turkey 2008," January 2009, Fig. 4 in the summary report; also Fig. 4.1, p. 49.

8. "He Loves You, He Beats You." Family Violence in Turkey and Access to Protection, Human Rights Watch, New York, 3. http://www.hrw.org/sites/default/files/reports/turkey0511webwcover.pdf

9. Turkish Civil and Penal Code Reforms from a Gender Perspective: The Success of Two Nationwide Campaigns, Women for Women's Human Rights (WWHR)—NEW WAYS February 2005. www.wwhr.org/images/CivilandPenalCodeReforms.pdf, 14.

10. Ali Çarkoğlu and Binnaz Toprak, *Religion, Society and Politics in a Changing Turkey* (Istanbul: Tesev Publications, 2007), 63 ff.

11. Aliye Kavaf, quoted in *Hürriyet Daily News*, March 7, 2010.

12. See Walter G. Andrews and Mehmet Kalpakli, *The Age of Beloveds: Love and the Beloved in Early Modern Ottoman and European Culture and Society* (Durham, NC: Duke University Press, 2005).

13. See the discussion of this in Hale Bolak Boratav, "Making Sense of Heterosexuality: An Exploratory Study of Young Heterosexual Identities in Turkey," *Sex Roles* 54, nos. 3/4 (February 2006), including references to the work of Deniz Kandiyoti.

14. Such linkage is a "red herring" according to a well-produced report by the European Stability Initiative: http://www.esiweb.org/index.php?lang=en&id=322&debate_ID=2&slide_ID=14

15. "The Trial Chamber found that, given the patriarchal character of the Bosnian Muslim society in Srebrenica, the destruction of such a sizeable number of men would 'inevitably result in the physical disappearance of the Bosnian Muslim population at Srebrenica.'" Proceedings Cited in the European Yearbook of Minority Issues, vol. 3, 2003/4 by European Centre for Minority Issues, June 2005, 127.

16. See Caroline Finkel, *Osman's Dream* (London: John Murray, 2005), 538–539.

17. Selim Deringil, "'The Armenian Question Is Finally Closed': Mass Conversions of Armenians in Anatolia during the Hamidian Massacres of 1895–1897," *Comparative Studies in Society and History* 51, no. 2 (2009):344–371.

18. The point is made poignantly in the angry 1929 memoir of Sarkis Torossian, a much-decorated captain in the Ottoman army who was wounded in the Gallipoli Campaign while his family from Central Anatolia was being deported to their deaths. From Dardanelle to Palestine, Boston: Meador, 1927 There were some 44,000 allied casualties of which 11,500 were from Australia and New Zealand. The Ottomans lost 86,500 soldiers (source: Australian Department of Veteran Affairs).

FURTHER READING

What follows is a simple guide to online sources and updates on Turkey-related issues. There is also an eclectic sampling of books about Turkey—both general and with some more specialized or classical studies of issues raised in this book. I have confined myself to English-language sources.

Remaining abreast with Turkish affairs:

Newspapers and news agencies

Anadolu Agency (http://www.aa.com.tr/en)—*Semi-official.*
Bianet (http://bianet.org/english)—*Independent, sketchily edited, often insightful and more left-wing.*
Hürriyet Daily News (www.hurriyetdailynews.com)
There are two English-language newspapers in Turkey, both with print and online additions, both with strengths and weaknesses. Reading a Turkish newspaper is an acquired skill (see my "Why Turkish Newspapers Sometimes Lie," below).
Today's Zaman (www.todayszaman.com)

Occasional papers, series, software

European Stability Initiative (http://www.esiweb.org) —*Produces discussion papers on key aspects of Turkish society.*
German Marshall Fund of the United States, On Turkey Policy Brief Series (http://www.gmfus.org/onturkey)—*Produces regular analyses of current affairs.*

International Crisis Group: http://www.crisisgroup.org/en/regions/
europe/turkey-cyprus/turkey.aspx—*Produces detailed analysis of
key domestic and international issues.*
Ogranisation for Economic Co-operation and Development—*OECD
Publishing produces annual economic surveys on Turkey as well as
occasional studies—e.g., Review of Health Systems 2008, Energy 2009,
Agricultural Reform 2011.*
Turkey Data Monitor (http://www.turkeydatamonitor.com)—
*Downloadable subscription (English and Turkish, though website
currently only Turkish) designed more for the corporate or academic user;
enormous amount of information packaged in a very friendly format.*

Blogs:

Istanbul Analytics by Murat Üçer and Atilla Yesilada, http://www.istan
bulanalytics.com—*Less a blog than an online newsletter with political
and international developments, and economic news.*
Istanbul Calling by Yigal Schleifer, http://istanbulcalling.blogspot.
com—*Seasoned commentary—though his work increasingly appears on
www.Eurasianet.org.*
Kamil Pasha by Jenny White, http://kamilpasha.com—*Covers a wide
range of topical, largely sociological issues.*

Books:

Berkes, Niyazi. *The Development of Secularism in Turkey.* Montreal: McGill
University Press, 1964.
Clark, Bruce. *Twice a Stranger: the Mass Expulsions That Forged Modern
Greece and Turkey.* Cambridge, MA: Harvard University Press,
2006.
Çetin, Fethiye, and Maureen Freely. *My Grandmother: A Memoir.* North
Melbourne, Vic.: Spinifex, 2010.
Finkel, Andrew, and Nükhet Sirman. *Turkish State, Turkish Society.*
London: Routledge, 1990.
Finkel, Andrew. "Why Turkish Newspapers Sometimes Lie." Reprint,
*Writing Turkey: Explorations in Turkish History, Politics, and Cultural
Identity.* Ed. Gerald MacLean. London: Middlesex University Press,
2006.
Finkel, Caroline. *Osman's Dream: The Story of the Ottoman Empire, 1300–1923.*
New York: Basic, 2006.
Göktürk, Deniz, Levent Soysal, and Ipek Türeli. *Orienting Istanbul:
Cultural Capital of Europe?* London: Routledge, 2010.
Hale, William, and Ergun Özbudun. *Islamism, Democracy and Liberalism
in Turkey: The Case of the AKP.* London: Routledge, 2010.

Hale, William M. *Turkish Foreign Policy, 1774–2000*. London: Frank Cass, 2002. New edition pending.

Hanioğlu, M. Şükrü. *Atatürk: An Intellectual Biography*. Princeton: Princeton University Press, 2011.

Kinzer, Stephen. *Crescent and Star: Turkey between Two Worlds*. New York: Farrar, Straus and Giroux, 2001.

Lewis, Geoffrey. *The Turkish Language Reform: A Catastrophic Success*. Oxford: Oxford University Press, 2010.

Lewis, Reina. *Rethinking Orientalism: Women, Travel, and the Ottoman Harem*. New Brunswick, NJ: Rutgers University Press, 2004.

Mango, Andrew. *Atatürk*. Woodstock, NY: Overlook, 2000.

Mansel, Philip. *Constantinople: City of the World's Desire, 1453–1924*. New York: St. Martin's, 1996.

Marcus, Aliza. *Blood and Belief: The PKK and the Kurdish Fight for Independence*. New York: New York University Press, 2007.

Mardin, Şerif. *The Genesis of Young Ottoman Thought. A Study in the Modernization of Turkish Political Ideas*. Princeton: Princeton University Press, 1962.

Mardin, Şerif. *Religion and Social Change in Modern Turkey: The Case of Bediüzzaman Said Nursi*. Albany: State University of New York, 1989.

McDowall, David. *A Modern History of the Kurds*. London: I. B. Tauris, 2004.

Öktem, Kerem. *Turkey since 1989: Angry Nation*. London: Zed, 2011.

Öniş, Ziya, and Barry M. Rubin. *The Turkish Economy in Crisis*. London: Frank Cass, 2003.

Özyürek, Esra. *The Politics of Public Memory in Turkey*. Syracuse, NY: Syracuse University Press, 2007.

Pamuk, Orhan. *Snow*. Trans. Maureen Freely. New York: Knopf, 2004.

Pope, Nicole, and Hugh Pope. *Turkey Unveiled: A History of Modern Turkey*. Woodstock, NY: Overlook, 1998.

Togan, Sübidey, and Bernard M. Hoekman. *Turkey: Economic Reform and Accession to the European Union*. Washington, DC: World Bank, 2005.

Üçer, Murat, and C. Van Rijckeghem. *The Turkish Financial Crises of 2000–01*. Istanbul: Bogazici University is the publisher Istanbul: Boğaziçi University, 2006.

Zürcher, Erik Jan. *Turkey: A Modern History*. London: I. B. Tauris, 2005.

INDEX